THURSDAY'S
DAUGHTERS

THURSDAY'S DAUGHTERS

The Story of Women Working in America

by Janet Harris

Harper & Row, Publishers
New York, Hagerstown, San Francisco, London

I should like to thank the MacDowell Colony for the fellowship that enabled me to begin this book.

THURSDAY'S DAUGHTERS:
The Story of Women Working in America
Copyright © 1977 by Janet Harris

FIRST EDITION

Library of Congress Cataloging in Publication Data
Harris, Janet.
    Thursday's daughters.

    SUMMARY: A brief anecdotal history of the jobs
women have held and the struggles they have waged to
expand and improve their opportunities for employment.
    1. Women—Employment—United States—Juvenile
literature. [1. Women—Employment] I. Title.
HD6095.H37   1977   331.4′024′055   76-58724
ISBN 0-06-022233-6
ISBN 0-06-022234-4 lib. bdg.

To My Mother
Ida Lachow Urovsky
In Loving Memory

Contents

Monday's child is fair of face,
Tuesday's child is full of grace,
Wednesday's child is loving and giving,
Thursday's child works hard for a living.
Friday's child is full of woe,
Saturday's child has far to go,
But the child that is born on the Sabbath-day
Is brave and bonny, and good and gay.

THURSDAY'S
DAUGHTERS

1

A Major Revolution

The sun is high in the cloudless sky that arches over the Gulf of Mexico some eighty-five miles off the Louisiana coast. Its reflection dances off the metal on the Marlin 2, a barge-tender rig that floats next to a smaller platform where a group of workers is drilling an oil well deep in the Gulf's floor. Now and again one of the laborers, dressed in greasy coveralls and steel-toed shoes, adjusts a hard hat to keep off the glare; but like the men she works with in the offshore oil industry, Cindy Myers doesn't stop. There is too much to do.

Cindy Myers is a roustabout—a drilling-rig work-hand. Her job is hard: splicing cable, sandblasting, painting bulkheads. Her life on the barge tender is austere. The Marlin 2 is not fastened to the seafloor, and it bobs up and down on the waves, like a ship. There are two crews, and each works one full week on the rig; then helicopters fly them to shore for a week's break. Cindy shares a room with three female kitchen workers, or, as they are called at sea, galley hands. The room has its own toilet facilities and a lock on the door, although Federal guidelines require only a sheet to separate male and female sleeping areas.

Federal guidelines do more than set regulations concerning Cindy's living accommodations. Cindy holds what until recently was considered by industry and the general public a "man's job" because legislation enacted by the Congress of the United States in the years since 1964 has increasingly prohibited sex discrimination in employment. Companies, like those in the offshore oil industry, which hold Federal leases must make sure their hiring practices comply with regulations designed to prevent assigning jobs on the basis of sex, race, religion, or age. If they don't, they risk losing their contracts with the government.

In other parts of the country, too, other young women are beginning to penetrate what used to be considered men's fields before the passage of the Federal Equal Employment Act of 1972. One such pioneer is Kathy Richter, who traded her job as a secretary to wield a drill at the Chevrolet Gear and Axle plant in Detroit.

Like Cindy Myers, whose previous job was in light industry, Kathy Richter found her new work challenging, difficult, and somewhat discouraging at first. Her hands weren't hardened to working with rough, splintery steel parts. A foreman who resented her because she was a woman assigned her the hardest job—unloading heavy truck axles—in the hope that she would quit during her ninety-day probationary period. But she stuck it out, toughened up, and got ready to deal with the next round of difficulties.

4

Kathy Richter is luckier than many working women, for she is a member of the United Automobile Workers union. The UAW has what are generally considered among the best contractual protections for women in the country. But according to Lillian Hatcher of the UAW's women's department, sex discrimination "at the hiring gate" is hardly a "thing of the past." As in other industries, the order of preference in engaging new help in the automotive field is white male, black male, white female, black female. United States Labor Department statistics showed that at the end of 1975 about eighteen out of one hundred of the country's blue-collar workforce were female—only three percent higher than it was in 1960.

In Boston, Massachusetts, there is another woman who works in a predominantly male domain. She is Sally Humery, and she is a district manager in the information-systems divisions at Honeywell, Inc.—a job requiring her to coordinate a team of sixteen male engineers who keep her company's computers running.

Sally Humery has a bachelor of science degree in mechanical engineering from the University of Wisconsin. When she graduated, in 1960, she was one of 18 women among 2,586 engineering students. Fifteen years later, the school's enrollment of 2,629 included 186 women. Sally Humery is part of a growing number of women moving into management positions in American industry. According to the Equal Employment Opportunity Commission, the total number of women officials and managers at companies with more than one hundred employees increased from 9.2 million in 1966 to 12.6 million in 1973.

On Sally Humery's desk there is an avocado plant which she tends with care, but on the wall outside the office there's a picture of Vince Lombardi with the football coach's description of "What it takes to be No. 1." She thinks that as a woman she faces problems that she would not have if she were a man. "If there's anything a woman in management needs to do differently from a man," she explains, "it's to learn not to react as fast [because people] expect her to react emotionally. Which is only because most of the situations men have been in with women before have been emotional— mothers or wives or sweethearts."

Why, then, in view of the difficulties—discriminatory hiring patterns, harder work, longer hours—would women like Kathy Richter and Cindy Myers want to work with forges and presses, drills and lathes? Why would young women like Sally Humery attempt to penetrate traditionally male preserves such as engineering and business management? Why would they bring suit in antidiscrimination cases through agencies such as the Equal Employment Opportunity Commission, or join together to see that affirmative-action guidelines, established throughout the country by state, county, and local governments to insure that women will have equal pay and equal opportunity for advancement, are enforced? Why, indeed, would women today—in a myriad of other ways—step out of what is traditionally the feminine role?

Listen to Kathy Richter's explanation: "After four years as a secretary I was making $3.85 an hour, and I started out here, at Chevrolet, at $4.85." Kathy's present salary is $6.60 an hour—or $264.00 a week, before overtime. Cindy's reasons for moving out of "women's work"—assembling parts for fans on an assembly line—are very nearly the same. With a low-paying job she could not afford to pay room and board and installments on the car she needed to drive to work. Now her checks for two weeks' work average out to over $400—enough to support a single woman comfortably. Sally Humery's reasons are equally to the point. "I've always worked," she explains. "It was a necessity." She supported her family while her husband was in medical school, and now that she is separated, she maintains a home for her two children. "Women have always worked. That's really not the issue. The issue is letting women earn a decent living for their work."

Kathy Richter, Cindy Myers, and Sally Humery, *like the vast majority of women in the working force today, work for the very same reasons that men do. They must support themselves and/or contribute to a family economic unit.* For that reason their wages, chances for advancement, fringe benefits such as pensions, health plans, unemployment coverage, are as important to them as such concerns have always been to men in our society, and for that reason they are willing to buck tradition, put themselves on the line in what, until now, society has largely considered a "man's world."

Who are today's working women? The answer, surprisingly, is: more than half of all women in America between the ages of eighteen and fifty-five! Despite the fairy tale that tells her that she will "marry and live happily ever after," today's schoolgirl is likely to spend at least twenty years employed outside her own home, and in work where she will receive a paycheck. The greater part of the female workforce is married: some 51 percent, as compared with 49 percent who are single, widowed, divorced, or separated. Moreover, 21 percent of the female working force are in marriages where the principal wage earner, the husband, earns less than ten thousand dollars a year. The only two substantial groups of women not largely represented in the working community are women over sixty and mothers of preschool children. But even in this last group—the women whom the popular image has most closely tied to home and hearth—almost one third work outside the home. Taken as a whole, women currently make up some 40.7 percent of the labor force. This is a figure that rose sharply during the last decade, and gives every indication of further spiraling upward.

A woman is most likely to work between the time she leaves school and marries, and then again when her children are in school full time. Black or other minority women are more likely to work outside the home than their white sisters. Although the majority of married women hold paid outside employment, a far greater percentage of single, widowed, divorced, or separated women work. Paradoxically, while the chances of a woman's working are higher if her family unit is in the lower economic brackets, there is also a relationship between higher education and work. Women who are college graduates, or have postgraduate degrees, are the most likely members of the labor market. Nearly 80 percent of all women with advanced degrees are presently working or are looking for jobs.

The composite picture of today's working woman is very different from the old stereotype that divided wage-earning women into three groups: the young woman who worked for a few years until "Mr. Right" came along; the hard-bitten career woman who renounced marriage and children in a pitched battle with men to climb to the top; the daughter of a poverty-stricken family who labored in a mill or as a domestic to earn the few dollars to keep body and soul together. In this last quarter of the twentieth century, for the first time in American history, women from all walks of life have taken their places as members of the working force. This change has come not in response to a temporary emergency—such as wartime mobilization—but as part of a long-term series of developments that have suddenly gained their own momentum. The new presence of millions of women in the workforce is the result of major transformations in the home, the school, the labor market, and the larger culture. It is, in turn, reshaping the American economy and the very fabric of life itself.

Men's work has always related directly to the economy. In an agricultural society most men farm the land; in a society of commerce and small trade, such as in Colonial New England, men became craftsmen or storekeepers, built ships or crewed them; in an industrial society men work with machinery or in management. Behind all Americans—both men and women—lies a common heritage. There is the legacy of a Puritan society, in which idleness was a moral sin as well as an economic liability. There were the needs of the frontier for every available hand to clear forests, build homes, farm the land. The nineteenth century brought industrialism—the substitution of mills and factories for home industry. To train people in an industrial society there was the development of a massive public-education and land-grant-college system. The Civil War brought America from trade and farms to commerce and industry, and the beginning of the twentieth century introduced the telephone, typewriter, and telegraph, the railroad, and eventually the automobile—a tight web of transportation and communication that linked the nation, making it a great commercial and industrial power. There were the booms and busts of inflation and depression, wars and reconstruction, and now, in the present revolution—cybernetics and computer technology.

Women's place in society goes far beyond the economic forces that shape male employment. There is a whole range of factors—social, religious, moral, beliefs about biology and anatomy—that play their part. First, there are beliefs about marriage and parenthood, for woman's role in all societies relates first to the position she fills as wife and mother. What is the proper age for marriage? How large should a family be? Can a woman control the size of her family? Should she? What about premarital chastity? Fidelity after marriage? If a woman goes into the marketplace to work, what will happen to her morality? How should her children be educated? Should they remain at home with her, or go out to school? How about her health and vitality? Is she physically strong enough to work outside the home? Should she be protected by special laws? Will work interfere with her ability to bear children? What about her intelligence, ability? Is she disfavored by nature by being less rational, more emotional, less scientific, less mathematically inclined?

For more than three hundred years—since the first ship that brought Englishwomen to the colony of Jamestown dropped anchor—these and other questions have been debated. Caught between the requirements of a burgeoning capitalist economy with its need for vast labor pools—the ever increasing industrialism that has made America the most powerful, productive, and prosperous nation in the history of the world—and the traditional forces that have sought to keep women in the home, American women have attempted to forge a place of their own.

Behind the broad outlines of history are the women themselves: heroines, martyrs, ordinary citizens who lived lives of quiet anonymity. There is a whole panorama: indentured servants and Colonial innkeepers, mill girls and sweatshop "greenhands," immigrants from famine-struck Ireland and freedwomen from the South. There are schoolmarms in one-room schoolhouses and bluestockings in Female Academies, nurses at the war fronts, "lady authors," homesteaders, adventurous women going west with the railroads, the civilian army of Rosie the Riveters who "manned" the factories during World War II. Finally, there is today's woman who seeks to expand her opportunities, to choose work that reflects her ability and talents, and to place her own stamp on her time and place.

This is their story.

2

A Kind of Rough Equality

The first small band of settlers to land in 1607 on the marshy peninsula they named "James Citty" were men. The tedious journey from London took four months, and the place they chose for the first permanent colony in North America did not look promising. There were swamps, streams of brackish water, and strange-looking natives, "tall and straight . . . of a colour browne," whom the Englishmen called "Savages."

Adventurers rather than colonists, the men set about their first work. "The fourteenth day," Master George Percy wrote in his diary, "we landed all our men, which were to set to worke about the fortification . . . the fifteenth of June we had built and finished our Fort, which was triangle wise . . . having foure or five pieces of Artillerie mounted on it. We had made our selves sufficiently strong for these Savages."

The first ships that arrived in Jamestown harbor carried only men. Their names—the *Susan Constant*, the *Discovery*, the *Godspeed*, and the *Pioneer*—were prophetic, for when the colonists began to settle the land, to plant their crops and build their homes, they found that the pioneering of America would depend upon the courage and constancy of women. Men might build barricades; to build a new country they needed women.

The settlers appealed to the businessmen of London who had financed the Virginia venture. The response was quick. The canny bankers saw that if they were to realize a profit on the capital they had advanced for ships, tools, and other goods, they would need a stable community of farms and businesses, not a bivouac of warriors and adventurers. Advertisements were sent out: "Agreeable persons, young and incorrupt . . . sold with their own consent to settlers as wives, the price to be the cost of their transportation."

The Proceedings of the English Colonie in Virginia makes special mention of the arrival of Anne Forest, who came to join her husband in 1608: "The ships having disburdened her selfe of 70 persons, with the first gentlewoman and woman servant that arrived in our Colony. . . ." Other women followed and set to work alongside their menfolk to turn the armed camp into a colony. Within five years they saw results of their labors. Jamestown began to export goods back to England: "Masts, cedar logs, blacke wallnut, clapboarde . . . and Gould Oare," which unfortunately "proved dirt." Tobacco was planted, silkworms imported. The wilderness gave way to productive farms, flourishing lumber and small-manufacturing businesses, and "faire rowes of howses."

The men and women who first settled the Thirteen Colonies were a strange assortment. There were farmers and people in trade whose enterprises had failed, forcing them to emigrate or go to debtors' prison. There were "gentlefolk," the younger sons of wealthy landowners who were victims of the law of primogeniture—the rule that property is inherited by the oldest son. There were adventurers seeking their fortunes, beggars, orphans, criminals, prisoners of war. There were principled people who sought religious freedom in a new world. There were women of "uncertain means" and ambitious young girls who were willing to face hardship in the colonies with husbands they were yet to meet.

What all of the settlers had in common was the new country, a place of forests to be cleared, land to be plowed and reaped, plains to be built into villages and cities, rocky coasts to be made into seaports. All that was needed was willing hands to do the work.

The early settlers applied themselves to the problem at once. They brought indentured servants to the new land. Ships drew into coastal ports, heralded by announcements such as this one in the *Virginia Gazette*:

> Just Arrived at Leedstown, the Ship *Justitia*, with about One Hundred Healthy Servants. Men, Women and Boys, among which are many Tradepeople—viz. Blacksmiths, Shoemakers, Tailors, House Carpenters and Joiners, a Cooper, several Silversmiths, Weavers, a Jeweler, and many others. The sale will commence on Tuesday, the 2nd of April. . . .

The sale was likely to be made on these terms: A planter was granted 50 acres of land for each immigrant servant, and the indentured servants were sold to the landowners (or in some cases, to the colony) to work for a certain number of years, usually seven, to pay the price of their passage to America. After their period of bondage ended, they were given goods to start life independently, some land perhaps, tools of their trade, money, and clothes.

The terms of indenture were harsh for both sexes. The hours were "rising sun to setting sun," with five hours off during the "heat of the summer day" and on the Sabbath. There were special penalties for women, however. While a man might be publicly censured for not behaving according to the rigid moral codes of the colonies, if a servant girl gave birth to a child out of wedlock, the punishment was a longer term of bondage. "Late experiments shew that some dissolute masters have gotten their maides with child," a journal of the time regrets, "and yet claim the benefit of their services."

If the terms were harsh for the poor whites escaping debt or imprisonment in Europe, they were even harder for the unwilling immigrants who first arrived when a mysterious ship flying a Dutch flag put into Jamestown harbor in 1619 with a cargo of captured Africans.

Like the white bondservants, the black people at first labored under terms of indenture. For a time, black and white servants were traded on the open market, like food, clothing, and other goods. An old advertisement reads:

> Several Irish Maid Servants time most of them for Five Years. One Irish Man Servant Good Barber and Wiggmaker. Also Four or Five Likely Negro Boys.

15

But this state of affairs was not to last long. Unlike white servants, blacks could not run away and melt into the general population. As the plantations grew and cotton became the South's major product, needs for unskilled labor skyrocketed. The terms of black bondage became increasingly severe, and slavery became hereditary. Unlike whites, most black slaves could not buy their freedom. They had virtually no hope of becoming independent tradespeople or landowners themselves.

The wilderness developed into a series of colonies spread out along the Eastern seaboard: plantation owners and slaves in the South, farmers, small business owners, and a few well-to-do merchant-fleet owners and shipbuilders, mechanics, and artisans in the Middle Atlantic states and New England.

Except among the wealthy planters of the South, where a leisure class developed, the Colonial society tolerated no idleness. There was simply too much to be done. While there were some class distinctions—a group of New England town fathers went on record as declaring their "utter detestation and dislike that men and women of mean condition should take upon themselves the garb of gentlemen . . . wearing silver lace or buttons . . . or women of the same rank to wear silk or tiffany scarfs . . ."—there was a kind of rough equality between the sexes.

Both men and women worked hard, often side by side, doing the same kind of labor. "There shall be no man or woman," reads an early ecological law, passed in Jamestown in 1611, "Launderer or Launderesse, dare to wash any uncleane Linnen, or throw out the water or suds of fowle clothes, in the open streete." Black slaves, both men and women, worked together on the plantations as field hands, chopping cotton or stripping tobacco, or served as house servants; and whether the slave was to work all day in the hot fields or enjoy the comparative luxury and status of servitude in the main house depended on strength and intelligence—or the planter's whim—not on gender.

On the small Colonial farms both men and women planted, sowed, tilled and reaped, set hens, fed pigs, and milked cows. Besides clearing the land and working the fields—where women often took their babies to play in the furrows alongside of them—there were the domestic chores: making clothes for the family out of wool or flax that the women themselves had raised, spun, dyed, and woven; brewing; baking; curing; dipping candles. From old records, journals, newspaper accounts, a picture of the Colonial woman comes into focus. Janet Shaw, a Scotswoman who kept a diary about her visit to America before the Revolution, later published as *A Journal of a Lady of Quality*, describes a farm in Wilmington, North Carolina:

> They tell me that the Mrs. of this place is a pattern of industry, and that the house and everything in it was the product of her labors. She has a garden, from which she supplies the town with what vegetables they use, also with mellons and other fruits. She even descends to make minced pies, tarts and cheese-cakes, and little biskets, which she sends down to town once or twice a day, besides her eggs, poultry, and butter, and she is the only one who continues to have milk. They tell me she is an

agreeable woman, and I assume she has good sense—
all her little commodities are contrived so as not to
exceed one penny a piece.

Not all of the women on farms and plantations, even
in those days of hard scrounging for a living from the
soil, were poor. There was nothing to prevent women
from owning land on exactly the same terms as men. Like
the male colonists, some women were able to parlay land
grants or cheaply purchased acreage into sizeable fortunes.

There was Margaret Hardenbroeck Philipse, for example, who was called "perhaps the most enterprising of
all the Dutch Colonists, male or female." She came to the
New World with her first husband, Peter De Vries.
They bought a plantation on Staten Island and began a
settlement there. After her husband died, the widow
sold their property and invested the money in ships,
establishing the first packet line between Europe and
America. A shrewd trader, she commanded the utmost
respect from the businessmen with whom she dealt. By
the time she remarried—and with her second husband,
Frederick Philipse, who became her business partner,
built "Philipse Castle," which is presently a historical
landmark in Westchester—she was the richest woman in
New Amsterdam.

Even in the South, where legend would have us believe
women were frail flowers, there were women who
owned and operated huge plantations. It was a woman—
Elizabeth Digges—who owned 108 black slaves, the
largest number in the possession of one person in
seventeenth-century Virginia. Another woman, Eliza

Lucas of South Carolina, became a successful exporter: "I have planted a figg orchard," Eliza wrote to a friend in 1741, when she was only nineteen,

> with a design to dry them and export them. I have reckined my expense and the prophets [profits] to dry them and export . . . but was I to tell you how great an Estate I am to make this way, and how 'tis to be laid out, you would think me far gone in romance. Yr. good Uncle has long thought I have a fertile brain for schemeing, I only confirm him in his opinion; but I own I love the vegitible world extreamly.

Eliza's dreams may have been "romantic," but her life was full of practical accomplishment. She was the daughter of a British army officer who had advanced ideas about women. He refused to let her learn embroidery and crewelwork, women's occupations, instead encouraging her to read ancient Greek and modern French philosophers in their own languages. Eliza was left in full charge of the family plantation at seventeen, when her father rejoined his command at Antigua. The girl was more than up to the job. She began her experiments with "the vegitible world," developed a new strain of indigo, which was then the Carolinas' chief crop. Soon other plantation owners were anxious to buy her superior hybrid seed, and eventually Eliza's market extended throughout the South and abroad.

Margaret Philipse, Elizabeth Digges, and Eliza Lucas were well within the early American pattern of rewards according to achievement and hard work, not sex distinction. The gender of a farmer was irrelevant; there was no discrimination in the market when it was time to sell products, nor were employees, such as the North's "hired hands" or the South's overseers, less likely to seek employment from a woman than a man. Even as America began its transition from a primarily agrarian economy—one in which most people tended the land and lived off it—to a mercantile economy, one depending on trade and commerce, women moved easily into ownership of businesses on an equal level with men.

It was along the coast in the Middle Atlantic states and New England that the changeover from farm to business began. Shipping and shipbuilding, importing finished goods—and slaves—and exporting raw materials such as cotton, indigo, rice, and tobacco became major ventures. Towns, villages, and small cities began to grow. Retail shops, small manufacturing establishments, inns and eating houses were established.

At the center of the burgeoning commercial life of the colonies was the tavern, or inn. Travel was slow and sometimes dangerous, and traders who spent days on the road needed places to stay. Commerce was often conducted in inns and public houses, as it had been in Elizabethan England. While women rarely traveled for business reasons, tavernkeeping itself became the business of many women.

The names of the inns give hints about their clientele. "The Connestoga Waggon," owned by Mary Jenkins, must have been on a main road on a trail leading westward, while Margaret Berwick's "The Three Mariners" was probably a way station for men whose living came from the sea. We can almost see these women in their dark dresses and aprons, overseeing "chambers" and kitchens, keeping warm fires and welcome hearths for tired travelers, seeing to it that horses were quartered, tallying accounts at their high desks by candlelight after everyone else had gone to bed.

The innkeepers were capable women—they had to be, for even in a time when expansion of business seemed limitless, there was still competition. To entice their customers, they posted "publick notices" and ran advertisements in the local newspapers:

"The subscriber begs to inform the public," says an advertisement placed in 1762 by Sarah Randall of Philadelphia,

> that she has removed from the Sign of the Seige of Louisbourg, a little below the drawbridge, Philadelphia, to the House where Mr. Murray kept the Sign of the Salutation Tavern, upon Society Hill, and next door to Mr. Neiman's where she has a very commodious House, fit to entertain a large company of Gentlemen; like wise a very good Billiard Table.

Closer to home than inns were coffee houses. "For the Entertainment of Gentlemen, Benefit of Commerce and Dispatch of Business" reads an ad in the *Boston Evening Post* of December 8, 1775,

> a Coffee House is this day opened in King Street. All the Newspapers upon the Continent are regularly taken in, and several English Prints and Magazines are ordered. Gentlemen who are pleased to use the House, may, at any

Time of Day, after the manner of those in London, have Tea, Coffee or Chocolate and constant Attendance given by

> their humble Servant
> Mary Ballard.

Some Colonial women who kept inns and taverns moved on the fringes of the ruthless underworld of privateers and adventurers. Colonial taverns often served as auction houses, where real estate, used household goods, and the stocks of ships that were closing out were displayed and sold. In times of war—particularly during King George's War in 1744–48 and the Seven Years' War, 1756–63—it was the booty captured from French ships by pirates that was up for auction. Perhaps the crew of the ship captured and put up for auction on the "New Dock" in New York in August 1747 perished on the disputed seas, but the Widow Lawrence, who kept a nautical tavern, probably did well with the exotic cargo she advertised in the New York *Gazette*: "A parcel of Maracaibo and Caraccas Cocoa . . . Silks, Silver and Gold Lace, Drugs for Apothecaries and sundry sorts of other Goods."

Most goods were sold directly in small shops tucked into the commercial districts of the cities. Some of the shopkeepers were women, often widows who carried on businesses left to them by their husbands, but occasionally women who had set up their own ventures and owned the stores themselves. Some inherited the money needed for shops and stock from relatives, some hoarded their earnings as workers until they were able to become independent businesswomen. The women took their merchandising seriously—just as men did—in that bustling, expansive age.

Miss Ann Smith served notice in 1773 that she had "returned to Philadelphia from London with a handsome assortment of books, and set up a bookstore." In 1726, the Widow Gordon of Philadelphia was advertising tobacco, "London Cut" at two shillings and sixpence the pound. At about the same time, Mrs. Boydell of Boston had "choice green tea" for sale. Mary Campbell was advertising Cheshire cheese and the Widow Debrossess offered "Oil of Olives and Canary Wine at 6 shillings per Gallon." Despite the Puritan horror of "fancy dress and finery," women in the New World liked pretty things: In conservative Boston and Quaker Philadelphia, women merchants were able to sell "A Variety of Ivory and Bone Stick Fans, Women's Shoes and Goloshes, very neat . . . Black Velvet Necklaces, Masks, Hair Powder, Crown and Hard Soap and Very Fine Chocolates." There was a market for less glamorous merchandise, too: Hannah Breintnall let the readers of the *Pennsylvania Gazette* know that she could be found at "The Sign of the Spectacles," where there were "true Venetian green Spectacles for weak or watery eyes."

The first shops in Colonial America sold imported luxuries. The necessities of life were homemade. Soap was boiled in a vat behind the house, meat smoked in a windowless shed, dresses and trousers cut and stitched before the fire in the "keeping room." But as the colonies became less primitive, "bought" merchandise replaced the household items that farm people had once produced for their own use. A group of skilled artisans was able to craft goods so finely made that they could compete with those imported from the Old World. By the middle of the eighteenth century, there was a large enough market for American-made products so people like Mary Cahill could place a notice in the *Pennsylvania Gazette* advising that she

> makes and sells all sorts of gentlemen's caps, Leather & Etc. Also Ladies' and Children's Caps, Mantilets . . . Hoods, Bonnets with black bags and roses for gentlemen's hair or wigs; all of which she makes after the newest and neatest fashions, very cheap.

Woman artificers produced and sold products that were typically "women's work." Mrs. Mary Crabbe offered, through the *Boston Evening Post*, "all sorts of Drawing and Embroidering . . . either in Gold or Silver or plain." Other women were engaged in mending "Gentlemen's Knitt Jackets and breeches . . . fine laundering of laces, clear starching and dyeing." Philadelphia newspapers in 1741 and 1742 mention three different women who ran bakeries—"best pound cake, on order, one shilling a pound, material furnished by purchaser." There were pickles "put up in kegs for shipping," brews of "Cannaomon, shakeron and clovewater spirits, sold very cheap for cash," and delicacies such as "puddings and pickled Sheeps Tongues."

But women also did work that is usually associated with brawny men: They were soapmakers, candlemakers, coachmakers and ropemakers. In Boston, the village smithy was Mary Salmon, who "continues to carry on the business of horseshoeing . . . where all gentlemen may have their Horse shod in the best Manner, as also all sorts of Blacksmith's work done with Fidelity and Dispatch." Another contemporary worked in tin and other metals: "Tea-Kettles and Coffee-Pots, copper Drinking Pots and Brass and Copper Sauce-Pans."

None of the women recorded makes a stronger case for the equality of sexes in early America than Martha Turnstall Smith. Mistress Smith came to New York with her husband and established a whaling fleet, which she ran. Here is a note from her diary: "Jan., ye 16, 1707, My company killed a yearling whale, made 27 barrels. Feb., ye 4, Indian Harry, with his boat, strick a whale and could not kill it; called my boat to help him. I had but a third, which was 4 barrels."

Along with the growth of trade and commerce in such seaports as Boston, Newport, New York City, and Philadelphia, there was the development of the most important adjunct to business—the newspaper. Commercial news was essential to carrying on profitable business with England and the West Indies and other colonies. Rumors of war drove up the price of tobacco, tariffs imposed by Parliament affected Colonial shippers, storms at sea sank vessels—and business people needed to know these things to determine trade and prices. Newspapers were the only way to advertise goods for sale—household furnishings and foodstuffs, tools. The first newspapers were imported from England, but as the colonies developed their own presses, women moved swiftly into the field. According to historian Frederic B. Farrar, "The ten greatest 'newspapermen' of the Colonial period were women."

There was Mary Katherine Goddard, who managed two major revolutionary papers, the *Pennsylvania Chron-*

icle and the *Maryland Journal*. She was the first newspaper publisher to print the Declaration of Independence with the signers' names. Anne Franklin stayed with the newspaper business after her husband, James (Ben's older brother), died. Anne Catherine Green ran the *Maryland Gazette*. The *Virginia Gazette*, the *Connecticut Courant*, and the *South Carolina Gazette* were also among the papers with women at the helm. Earlier, while John Peter Zenger, a symbol of freedom of the press, spent ten months in jail awaiting trial, his wife, Catharina, ran his *New York Journal*.

The names of women printers and publishers appear often in Colonial historical accounts. Women quite dominated government printing in prerevolutionary days and during the war. Dinah Nuthead, the first American printer, established a press at St. Mary's, Maryland, in 1686. She moved to Annapolis, then the capital of the colony. Her license stated the press would be used only for forms for government business, except by special permission of the governor. Anne Franklin, too, like other newspaper publishers, also printed pamphlets and government forms. Just as businessmen brought their sons into the family industry, Anne Franklin apprenticed her daughters. She taught them well, for an observer left a report that the young women were "correct and quick compositors."

Our Colonial forebears were a record-keeping people: There were town records, court records, tax lists, wills, and family papers. From these, we are able to surmise a great deal about the society, but there are no accurate statistics to show how many women were actually engaged in business. The first Census Bureau study, "Women at Work," was based on figures gathered at the end of the nineteenth century. It states that of the total number of people who were merchants and retail dealers in 1900, only about 4.3 percent were women. From culling newspaper advertisements and announcements, tax lists, and other business data, experts estimate that during Colonial days there were at least twice as many. Perhaps one out of every ten merchants, importers and store-owners was a woman, to say nothing of the high percentage of women engaged in other kinds of commercial ventures. In general business, women were to be found buying and selling, suing and being sued, acting as administrators and executors and having power of attorney.

But there is more to the picture than statistics alone reveal. The truth is that while Colonial women had the same opportunities as men to make money, they were limited in other ways. The patterns that would later take form and serve to channel women into role-defined work during the next two centuries were already subtly present in America's first colonies.

Although many of the colonists had come to the New World to escape the religious dogma of the Church of England, they brought with them certain old-world convictions—among them that church affairs were purely the domain of men. While women in the colonies were considered more "spiritual" than men, purer in heart and mind, when it came to playing a dominant role in the religious life of the community the colonists subscribed to the traditional view that since the church hierarchy had been in the hands of men beginning with Christ's all-male disciples, it was best to exclude women completely. This practice had important political results, for it was not until after the Revolution that there was a separation of church and state.

The colonists brought with them the European practice of excluding women from higher councils in general. Women did not serve in any governmental capacity. There were no women governors, burgesses, magistrates. While literacy was considered necessary for both sexes—little girls as well as little boys were taught to read and write and do simple arithmetic—higher education was closed to women. The colonists were too practical a people to consign women entirely to the European view, as expressed by the French philosopher Jean-Jacques Rousseau: "The whole education of women ought to be relative to men. . . . To please them, to be useful to them . . . and to make life sweet and agreeable to them." There was far too much need for women's industry and energy in building the New World to allow women to be mere diversions for men. But enough of Europe went west with the colonists to justify denying women full intellectual equality.

In short, women in Colonial America were allowed to work in their homes and out of them, to own and manage shops and businesses, to make investments, trade on the open market, and even have sway over the high seas. What they were *not* permitted to do was make policy, have a voice in the laws under which they lived, be accorded the same dignity and respect for their individual achievements as men were.

Now and again a woman's voice was raised in protest. There are clues that even in those days of egalitarian expansion, women in business were excluded from some of the advantages men enjoyed. There is an open letter addressed to Peter Zenger in the *New York Journal* of January 21, 1733, and signed by "The Widdows of this city" that complains:

> We are House Keepers, Pay our Taxes, carry on Trade, and most of us are she-Merchants, and as we in some measure contribute to the Support of the Government, we ought to be Intitled to some of the Sweets of it; but we find ourselves entirely neglected, while the Husbands that live in our Neighborhood are daily invited to Dine at Court; we have the Vanity to think we can be full as Entertaining, and make as brave a Defence in Case of an Invasion and perhaps not turn Taile as soon as some of them.

The most eloquent protest did not come from the businesswomen; it was voiced by "bluestockings"—a small group of educated women like Mercy Warren, a close friend of George Washington's, or Judith Murray, the daughter of a delegate to the Massachusetts convention which ratified the Constitution. Educated at home by parents who believed that women's intellects were equal to men's, Judith Murray took up the banner for other women who did not have her advantages. It was unreasonable, she wrote in an essay published later in her life, to assume that nature

> hath yielded to one half the human species so unquestionable a mental superiority. . . . Will it be said that the judgment of a male two years old is more sage than that of a female's of the same age? I believe the reverse is generally observed to be true. But from that period what partiality . . . the one is

taught to aspire, the other is early confined and limited.

Better known today is Abigail Adams' letter to her husband, John, later to be the second President of the United States. Reminding her husband that the colonists sought separation from England in order to govern themselves, she pleaded that the rights to self-determination be extended to *women*, too: "If particular care and attention is not paid to the ladies," she wrote, "we are determined to foment a rebellion, and will not hold ourselves bound by any laws in which we have no voice or representation."

Abigail Adams' half-joking threat had little impact. America was in the throes of two revolutions, one political and military, the other economic, but neither would improve the lot of women for the next century. The American Revolution granted "liberty, justice, and equality" to men, but withheld the blessings of civil rights from women, while the Industrial Revolution ended the equality of the first frontier by putting men and women into competition against each other for jobs in industry. Women would take a giant step backward before they could begin to move ahead again.

3

Sent Into the Factory,
to Pine Away . . .

In the heady excitement of establishing a new republic—
the United States of America, now completely severed
politically from England in the wake of the Revolutionary War—the pleas for legal and political equality
for women were ignored. Under the Constitution only
white males were permitted to vote, and state constitu-
tions and local laws denied women civil rights—such as
rights to own property—as well as the franchise. More
directly, women were affected by another revolution
that had its beginnings in Europe—this one economic
rather than political.

For thousands of years, people throughout the world
had lived by the labor they performed with their own
hands. Human energy wielded the first tools. But the
beginning of the eighteenth century, the dawn of
science—physical as well as biological—brought the discovery of new kinds of power. Energy sources such as

coal for fuel, steam to power engines, and eventually electricity, petroleum, and the internal combustion system meant that vast quantities of goods could be produced cheaply and quickly.

England was the natural breeding ground for the new revolution. For several centuries, England had dominated the seas, establishing colonies—in America, Africa, Asia—controlling trade and commerce all over the world. Fortunes had been amassed by bankers, shipowners. Two or three centuries of capital accumulation—the treasure of the New World, a favorable balance of exports, such as wool woven on hand looms—made it possible to finance the use of the new inventions. When science provided the means for mass production through power-driven machinery, the money needed to build the factories, store the vast quantities of raw materials that the machines used, pay for the costly machines themselves, already was in waiting for investment.

The invention of the spinning jenny about 1764 brought a shift of wealth and ownership. The giant power-driven machines were too large, complicated, and expensive to be owned and operated by peasants and artisans in their own homes. Instead of families owning the means of production, the costs had to be spread. Corporations were formed. Shareholders put up part of the capital needed to buy equipment, and in return received stock in the company. New classes emerged: at the bottom, an ever increasing labor class—the men, women, and children who worked for wages to produce goods. To oversee them were managers, who did not necessarily own shares in the companies, but rather were employees of absentee owners. Factories became impersonal institutions, and the distance between those who owned the machines and those who operated them widened as the revolution spread.

The Industrial Revolution reached right down into the lives of people. It brought a vast shift in population. A migration began: Families moved from farms and villages to industrial cities. A youngster no longer studied with a master craftsman to learn a trade; instead, growing numbers of men, women, and children would leave their homes each day to take their places behind flying shuttles, water frames, and power looms.

At first, families kept their rural ways. They lived in houses on plots of land large enough to raise their own food, and they did not have to rely solely on wages. But as the factory system spread and became more centralized, less and less room existed in the cities for gardens. Food was grown on farms away from the factories and shipped in, and if there were no wages because of unemployment, layoffs, recessions, or for other reasons, a family faced starvation. Workers became entirely dependent upon their machines to earn their livings, and they soon were at the mercy of the industrialists who owned the machines and controlled their livelihoods.

Instead of freeing people from the hard toil of earning a living by backbreaking labor, industrialization brought new kinds of suffering. Workers labored long hours for small wages, and lived in squalid tenements. Worse than the working conditions, though, was the insecurity. There was no labor legislation, no welfare or social security, no unemployment benefits. One's bread and butter depended upon economic conditions beyond one's control. People were often thrown out of work by temporary shutdowns, depressions, or business failures. New machines were being developed to replace the work of many laborers with few.

One of the victims of England's Industrial Revolution was a writer named Charles Dickens. His father was locked up in Marshalsea prison for bankruptcy, and the boy went to work, tying and labeling pots of blacking in a warehouse for the pennies his mother needed to buy food. By the time he was in his teens Charles Dickens had seen all the abuses of the industrialized society. His books, among them *Pickwick Papers* and *Oliver Twist*, described this life in England, and when in 1844 mill owners in Lowell, Massachusetts, invited him to observe the burgeoning industrialism of the new country and to let the rest of the western world know what life was like in the factories and mill towns of New England, Dickens eagerly accepted.

Perhaps it was the comparison to Europe that made Charles Dickens so enthusiastic about what he saw in America. Like England, the American East Coast was rapidly becoming a textile center. Since 1790, when Samuel Slater had first harnessed water power to spin cotton at Pawtucket, Rhode Island, the spinning wheels and looms that had been fixtures in kitchens and keeping rooms of farmhouses had become obsolete. Power machinery was now used to spin and weave fabric. Dickens had expected to find a grimy, sooty city. Instead he saw a pleasant town, with brick factories rising unobtrusively amid the farmlands of northern Massachusetts.

Lowell was full of young women and girls. As early as 1800 there were already some one hundred thousand workers in the clothmaking industry, and a large percentage of them were women. In fact the first power loom in America, set up in Waltham, Massachusetts, in 1814, had been operated by Deborah Skinner. Each year more and more young women left the farm and fireside to earn their wages alongside their brothers in New England's mill towns.

The young women's charm and liveliness fascinated Dickens. He compared their high spirits and obvious good health with the pinched, sallow look of English mill women, and wrote approvingly of "their neat bonnets over carefully curled ringlets, silk stockings . . . and parasols." He was delighted to find them "all well dressed, but not to my thinking above their station. . . . From all the crowd I saw in the different factories, I cannot recall or separate one face that gave me a painful impression."

Dickens inspected their living quarters, too. Lowell was a model community. It drew its labor force from the nearby farm country and the coastal villages of New England. In order to entice the farmers' and seamen's daughters to leave home and work for wages, the mills offered a total life—housing, food, and recreation.

The young women lived in special boarding houses, where there was strict supervision, in keeping with the morality of the times. A chaperone lived in each house. The doors closed at ten o'clock. The young women were expected to attend church, while the men with whom they worked were warned not to be "wanting in proper respect to the females employed by the company," nor to "smoke within the company's premises or be guilty of inebriety."

But in spite of the paternalistic rules (or perhaps because of them) the young women's living conditions seemed pleasant to Dickens. They were put up in "well-ordered rooms." There were "plants growing in windows, fresh air, cleanliness and comfort." More than that, Dickens noted that the employers offered something beyond mere room and board. It was—a dream, a hope for improvement. The women were lured to work in the mills by the promise that they could rise above their places as members of the working classes into the special world of cultured aristocracy.

Dickens described these benefits glowingly. There were, he wrote, in each of the lodging houses, "joint stock pianos." Nearly all the houses subscribed to circulating libraries and magazines. There was even a magazine, *The Lowell Offering*, to which the workers were encouraged to submit articles and stories. Viewing all the advantages of factory work in America, Dickens decided that it was a vast improvement over Europe's. The women, he concluded, "looked like human beings, not like beasts of burden."

Undoubtedly the lot of working women in the mills of New England was better than that of old England's, and some of Dickens' observations were correct. When the mills were first built, there were advantages for the women who left farms for paid employment. The work was lighter than the endless tasks of housework, farm work, and homecrafts. Life on the farm was a matter of dawn-to-dusk labor, and so the thirteen-hour factory day did not seem bad. The work was not so tedious and lonely, either. The young women could rest, read, and talk among themselves. Although wages were low, living expenses were reasonable, and the dollar or so that the workers could put aside each week bought pretty clothes and small luxuries in those days. Then, too, there was the sense of independence that the women found as wage earners. "They could earn money and spend it as they pleased," a girl in the Lowell mill explained. "They were no longer obliged to finish out their faded lives a burden to their male relatives."

But for all their independent spirit and high energy, the young women who spun and wove textiles in Lowell and Fall River, or stitched shoes in Lynn, or worked in the paper mills in Holyoke, had much going against them. To begin with, women in the labor force had little experience with wages generally. In Colonial America, young men apprenticed and learned trades, or worked as employees in small businesses, but women worked either as entrepreneurs—owners of their own businesses such as shops or inns—as domestics, or in homecrafts, where the price of goods sold rather than wages for producing them represented earnings. Until the textile and paper mills brought large numbers of women into the workforce, there was virtually no female labor class.

When the Industrial Revolution began, and throughout the years when times were good and there were enough jobs for everyone, the differences in the value of men's and women's work was not appreciable. But when times were hard, and competition for jobs in industry increased, employers discovered they could bring in untrained workers, mostly women, at lower wages. By pitting worker against worker, they could reduce the wages of both men and women.

Certain jobs became "feminized." In the shoe industry,

the work was carefully divided into men's work and women's work. In New England's early days, shoemaking was a home industry. Farmers who tilled the fields in summer made shoes in the winter: The men cut, lasted, and attached the soles in the small shops that were set up in towns, while the women who stayed at home with the children bound shoes in their kitchens or parlors. When industry came to New England, shoemaking became specialized, requiring between seventy and eighty "hands" to make each pair. Men continued to cut the leather and attach the uppers to the soles, while women were given lesser jobs—stitching the linings, vamps, and uppers, cleaning and polishing the finished shoes, and packing them into boxes. Once a job was designated as women's work, it became downgraded, and brought a lower salary and less status than men's work.

The "feminization" process spread from industry to industry. When factories, later, began to manufacture finished garments—suits and coats, for example—pattern makers and cutters continued to be male, while the actual sewing of the garments was deemed "women's work"— and brought with it correspondingly lower salaries. This "feminization" process in time became a general rule even in the professions. Today social work and public-school teaching, fields dominated by women professionals, bring much less remuneration than accounting and engineering, which are primarily masculine occupations.

Each year the gap between the value of men's and women's labor widened. As machinery became more specialized, women were assigned to the "lighter" tasks— with the excuse that they were "not fitted by nature" to bear the heavy loads that men were given. The fact that both sexes worked in the same poorly ventilated, primitively equipped factories—there were no lunchrooms, for example, and workers ate sitting either on the floor or on window ledges, fire escapes, or boxes—was not considered. Nor was it considered that both men and women worked the same sixty-five- or seventy-hour work week. Under the guise of "protecting women," the "weaker sex" was assigned to the least-skilled and therefore lowest-paying work.

As early as 1829, farsighted observers began to record the plight of the working woman. The *Boston Courier* observed:

> Custom and long habit have closed the doors of very many employments against the industry and perseverance of women. She has been taught to deem so many occupations . . . made for men only that . . . the competition for the few places left open to her has occasioned a reduction in the estimated value of her labor.

As a result, the editorial continued, women's wages had "fallen below the minimum" and could no longer provide a comfortable living for the worker, much less "the necessary provision against age and infirmity."

Another newspaper in 1833 stated that women earned only one fourth of men's wages, while a Philadelphia paper in the same year observed that the city's working women "did not receive as much wages for an entire week's work of 13 to 14 hours a day as journeymen receive in the same branches for a single day of 10 hours."

By the 1840's women worked an average of seventy-five hours a week, and after room and board were taken out of their meager wages earned an average of less than $1.50 a week. When the manager of one mill at Holyoke, Massachusetts, found his hands "languorous" because they had eaten breakfast, he ordered them to come to work on empty stomachs. "I regard my work people just as I regard my machinery," an agent at another factory said. "So long as they can do my work for what I choose to pay them, I keep them, getting out of them all I can."

Actually, the "work people" were treated more impersonally than machinery. "You furnish your operatives with no more healthy sleeping-apartments than the cellars and garrets of the English poor," the *Voice of Industry*, a new labor newspaper, told mill owner Abbot Laurance.

> The keepers are compelled to allow . . . but one room for 6 persons and generally crowd 12 into the same hot, ill-ventilated attic . . . allow them but a half hour to eat their meals . . . compel them to stand so long at the machinery that varicose veins, swelling of the feet and limbs . . . are not rare but common occurrence."

The mill hands, overworked and underpaid, uncertain of any work at all during times of recession and lay-offs, began to grow restive. Clearly, something had to be done.

The first rumblings came from an unlikely group of women—the "homeworkers." Not all of the women in the new textile industry worked in factories. There were thousands of women who did their sewing and finishing in their slum flats, often with their little children working alongside them at the less-skilled work—removing bastings or picking up scraps of cloth and thread. These women homeworkers worked for pitifully small wages—perhaps $1.25 a week. Their desperation led them to become the first group to seek joint action. They formed quaintly named organizations during the 1830's: the United Tailoresses Society of New York and the Lady Shoe Binders of Lynn, Massachusetts.

The homeworkers tried valiantly to set standards to benefit themselves and, for that matter, all working women. But they were handicapped. Although they shared a common cause, they worked in isolation from each other. The societies met for a time and then were disbanded, with not much to show for their efforts.

The "tailoresses" and "lady shoe-binders" could only brood alone over their grievances. The situation was different in the mills and factories. Each morning throngs of young women filed through the factory gates together, shared talk and food at lunch. They could congregate in small groups, secretly, in each other's rooms, and eventually openly in meeting halls. They began to talk about what was happening to them as wage earners, and to plan the steps they could take to help themselves.

The women had little background with which to forge a protest movement. They were inexperienced in organizing—although for that matter, so were men. While there had been rudimentary efforts at collective bargaining by men since Colonial days, the fledgling unions were composed only of skilled journeymen who would get together on some temporary basis to press demands and take a joint action to protect their interests.

In the textile industry, the beginnings of collective bargaining were sporadic attempts by women to band together against specific grievances. Men and women were on the early factory strike lines in Dover and Manchester, New Hampshire, and in Paterson, New Jersey. Angered by wage cuts or layoffs, workers would leave the mills, listen to speeches, stage a parade, and then, a few days later, dribble back to work. Perhaps the most dramatic of those early demonstrations was in Lowell, Massachusetts, in 1836. Hundreds of women millworkers marched through town singing:

Oh, isn't it a pity, such a pretty girl as I
Should be sent into the factory, to pine away and die?
Oh, I cannot be a slave,
I will not be a slave,
For I'm so fond of liberty
That I cannot be a slave.

Sometimes the strikers won their demands. Other times the mill owners held out, punishing the "troublemakers" and offering no rewards in exchange for concessions on the part of the laborers. At last, one cold December evening in 1844, the first group of women met in Lowell not to protest a single wrong, but to build a stable organization, develop leadership, and conduct a systematic campaign to improve the lot of all working women.

The Lowell mill hands were lucky, for among them was Sarah Bagley. Miss Bagley came to Lowell from New Hampshire, "a common schooled New England factory operative" as she described herself, sometime after the unsuccessful demonstration of 1836. For a time she was happy in her work. She joined one of the Improvement Circles, and she even wrote a paper on "The Pleasures of Factory Life." But slowly, as she explained to the women in the little group, she began to see that all the "pretty flower beds" outside the factory dormitories did not make up for the sudden cuts in wages, the longer hours, the unemployment during recessions. Unless women planned more lasting methods of redressing their grievances than periodic "turnouts," there was little hope that factory work would grow more secure or better paid.

With the encouragement of her friends, Sarah Bagley went to work organizing. The word spread among the mill hands, and soon there were fifty, a hundred, and finally, in May of 1845, six hundred members of the Female Labor Reform Association in Lowell, ready to band together under the motto "Try Again!"

Sarah Bagley was shrewd enough to see that although it was women who suffered most in the mills, they would have the most power if they did not isolate themselves from male workers. She wooed the heads of various reform groups that sprang up in the 1840's—coalitions of workingmen, artisans, and small businessmen—by telling them that "in unity there is strength." The New England Workingmen's Association responded by giving her space in their publication, the *Voice of Industry*.

Writing in a tone unusual for a woman of her time, she thundered at the textile companies who tried to blacklist employees for joining her group:

What! Deprive us, after working thirteen hours, of the poor privilege of finding fault—of saying our lot is a hard one! Intentionally turn away a girl unjustly

43

persecuted, as men have been persecuted . . . for free expression of honest political opinions. . . . We will make the name of him who dares . . . stink with every wind . . . and he shall be hissed in the streets . . . in all the cities of this widespread republic; for our name is legion though our oppression be great.

"All of the cities of this widespread republic" was an exaggeration—but it was certainly true that the Female Labor Reform Association soon spread to other New England towns. Sarah Bagley visited chapters in Manchester, Waltham, Dover, Nashua, Fall River. She brought other women in to work with her, taught them how to deal with the men leading the New England labor movement, and sent them as delegates to labor conventions. In 1846, three women became directors of the New England Labor Reform League—along with five men. Women at last seemed to be on their way to becoming a force in the trade unions.

Under Sarah Bagley's direction, the Lowell group steered its members into tactics that worked. When a mill tried to force each worker to handle four looms instead of three, at the same time reducing wages, the Association got nearly every woman weaver to sign a pledge vowing not to work more without an increase in pay. The mill canceled the speedup and acknowledged that the women had won.

Encouraged by their success, the leaders of the Association decided to go a step farther. Although women had no citizenship rights—it would be more than half a century before they could even vote—the Association's members joined the trade union movement in petitioning the Massachusetts state legislature to enact laws limiting the working day to ten hours.

Teams of mill women took petitions door to door. They produced so many signatures that the legislature was finally compelled to appoint a committee to investigate conditions in the mills. Eight millworkers were summoned as witnesses—six of them women.

The committee—the first ever to hold a state investigation into labor conditions—heard hard facts from Miss Bagley and her associates. Eliza Hemingway, a highly paid wool weaver, told about the room in which she worked. It was so overcrowded and poorly ventilated that sometimes as many as thirty women were sick in one day from the fumes of the oil lamps. Another woman testified that her health had been broken in the mills. She lost one year out of seven through illness.

Although the women prepared their testimony carefully—they even counted the number of oil lamps in each room—the legislators remained unconvinced. Like Charles Dickens two years earlier, they journeyed to Lowell and were taken in by the pretty landscaping outside the mills. They decided that "the intelligent and virtuous men and women" who had testified could be counted on to take care of themselves. There was no need for governmental regulations, they voted. The ten-hour day was out, and workers went back to the old conditions.

Labor, in general, fell upon hard times. Ireland's potato crop failed in 1845, and then again in 1846. The country's population declined from eight to six million. Those who did not starve or die of plague fled the country. Irish immigrants crowded the steerages of boats headed for New York, Boston, and Philadelphia. Soon the streets of the cities teemed with new Americans—unfed, unlettered, unskilled, and willing to work for pennies a day.

Industrialists, overjoyed with the influx of cheap labor, sought to break the backs of the unions. Congress, in 1864, cooperated by passing a contract labor law that bore some resemblance to the old indentured-labor system: Passage money was advanced to immigrants in return for a guarantee that it would be paid back out of their wages. Other immigrants came in waves, and with such steep competition women workers found their jobs jeopardized, their wages cut, their hours increased.

The "greenhands," as the newly arrived immigrants were called, swelled the numbers of women in industry. In 1850 there were about 226,000 women factory workers, 271,000 by 1860, and more than 323,000 by 1870. Five million immigrants between 1880 and 1890 skyrocketed the female labor force. The two and a half million women who worked in 1880 became more than four million ten years later—and working women accounted for nearly one fifth of the total American labor force.

Time after time women attempted to close the gap that separated men's work—with its more promising opportunities and better wages—from the underpaid, insecure, stopgap labor that was available to them. Often the handicap was the steep competition between male and female workers that the employers encouraged in order to keep everyone's wages down. Augusta Lewis, a typesetter who became an official in Local 6, New York's first printing union—originally an all-male organization—hit the nail on the head. She took the job in the hope of spanning "the chasm that has heretofore divided the interests of the male and female printers." But when the chips were down, she found, the male trade unionists were not able to see women as co-workers. "We refuse to take the men's situations when they are on strike," Miss Lewis wrote bitterly, "and when there is no strike if we ask for work in union offices we are told by union foremen that 'there are no conveniences for us.'"

Not all trade unionists failed to see the connection between securing rights for women and improving the lot of working people generally. Radical, foresighted William Sylvis, one of the founders of the short-lived National Labor Union, thought that the plight of working women was as serious as that of the other two disadvantaged groups whose cause he took up—convict laborers and black Americans newly freed from slavery. He pledged his undivided support to "the sewing women and daughters of toil in this land." Putting his theories into action, he insisted that Kate Mullany, president of the Collar Laundry Union of Troy, New York, be made assistant secretary of the NLU. But although women had a platform with the NLU, and a charter that linked their working rights with those of their brothers, they were largely unsuccessful in their early labor attempts. Sylvis died suddenly in 1869; the union vanished almost overnight. It was not until the Knights of Labor began organizing men and women on an equal basis in 1881 that women were again even able to have a forum.

The women brought their own style into the organization. Listen to Mrs. George Rodgers, the head of the

Knights' order in Chicago.

Tucking her youngest, a three-week-old baby, under her arm—there were eleven more children at home!—Mrs. Rodgers explained to an interviewer at the national convention, "I was the first woman in Chicago to join the Knights. They offered us the chance, and I said to myself, 'There must be a first one, so I'll go forward.'" When the interviewer asked how she spoke to the men delegates, Mrs. Rodgers replied easily, "Oh, just as I do to my children at home. I have no time to get anything ready to say, for I do . . . all my own work. I just talk as well as I can at the time."

The most eloquent spokeswoman was Irish-born Leonora Barry. Her education was sketchy, and she never lost her brogue, but when she spoke or wrote, the vividness of her words struck straight at the heart of her audience.

Mrs. Barry became a factory hand out of necessity. "I was left, without knowledge of business . . . work . . . or what the world was, with three fatherless children looking to me for bread." She mixed rhetoric with hard fact: "I speak of the contract-sweating middleman or slop-shop plan which works ruin, misery, sin and shame to toilers," and then went on to document her complaints: "Men's pants," she explained, "that retail at prices from $1 to $7 a pair are taken by the contractor at 15 cents per pair. Operatives are then employed and huddle together in a close, stifling backroom . . . and do all the machine work for 5 cents a pair." She spoke of working women as "victims," and in her most impassioned pleas begged the Knights of Labor "by your love for mothers, sisters, wives and daughters . . . unite as one man . . . to remove this curse of our fair land."

But although Leonora Barry railed at workingmen's inability to see women as co-workers, and at businesses' exploitation of women and children, she was realistic enough to know that women themselves were part of the problem. Her attempts to organize them were disappointing. She blamed "the habit of submission and acceptance" that women were taught.

> Every effort has been made to perfect and extend the organization of women, but our effort has not met with the response that the cause deserves— partly because those who have steady employment, fairly good wages, and comfortable homes do [nothing] to assist their less fortunate co-workers.

Worse still, as she knew from her own life that marriage was no guarantee of security for women, she regretted those "in the flush of womanhood" who held "the hope and expectancy that in the near future marriage will lift them out of the industrial life to the quiet and comfort of a home; often finding, however, that their struggle has only begun when they have to go back to the shop for two instead of one."

Leonora Barry's resignation from the union in 1890— she remarried and moved to St. Louis—came at a time of low ebb for the organization, and she was never replaced. Although women organized sporadically until the end of the century, they finally had little to show for their efforts.

After a full century of mill and factory labor, women

had failed to gain parity on the wage market. But another opportunity to move ahead was at hand. As industry spread technology advanced, became more sophisticated, creating a need for a pool of workers educated to deal with abstract concepts. Theories of education began to undergo revision: Learning beyond the basics of literacy was no longer an indulgence of the upper classes; it was rapidly becoming a necessity for the working classes. To instruct the children of the poor along with the children of the rich meant that there would have to be a vast army of professionally trained teachers. Women sensed that the time was right for them to fill the gap, but first they would have to open doors that had been closed to them since America's founding—the barriers to higher education.

4

Opening the Doors
to Equal Education

The needs of a complex industrial society are different from those of a society in which people draw their livings from the soil. No longer could America rely on a small group of schoolmasters and schoolmistresses whose own educations were either sketchy or heavily centered around the classics or religion. Modern industry meant modern education—scientific, technological learning—and a need to educate the women who would work in industry as well as the women who would prepare coming generations for industrial positions.

America had always been committed to the idea of educating its citizens. In both Holland and England popular education had been important, and the settlers who came from those countries resolved that the new world they were making would outshine the old. The first elementary school in New Amsterdam opened in 1633. The English colonies followed suit in Boston in

1635. In 1642 the legislature in Massachusetts passed a law requiring all parents and masters of children—worded to include young bondservants as well as natural offspring—to see to it that their charges were taught reading; the capital laws, those rules of conduct that were enforced by the colony's courts; religious catechism; and apprenticeship in a trade. Five years later the colony set up the machinery. Every town of fifty or more families was required to appoint a teacher of reading and writing, to be paid out of general funds "if the people so ordered."

The Colonial settlers were practical people. They knew that in order to survive, their children would have to learn to read and write and "cypher"—add and subtract—and how to earn their livings at their trades. Most important, the young people who were to make the New World had to have strong moral character. The 1647 Massachusetts law warned that "the oulde deluder, Satan" wanted to "keepe men from the knowledge of the scriptures." The colonists hoped to spite the devil by teaching their youngsters to read the Bible, to learn good and distinguish it from evil, to become not necessarily scholars and artists, but decent, God-fearing citizens.

The early schools set the pattern. Since the purpose of education was to instruct young people to uphold the values of the time, the schools reinforced what the colonists believed was right and proper for men, and also what was right and proper for women. The rub was that each sex had to follow a different path.

Colonial education was tied to religion, for not until after the Revolution was the separation of church and state enforced. The colonists believed that women were the weaker vessels, and that the Bible taught that women were to be subservient to men. The first sinner was Eve, and all subsequent generations of women were expected to pay the dues. Following the precepts of the Bible as they understood them, and also the heritage of "female" education in Europe, the colonists deemed education of the mind "improper and inconsistent" for girls. From the beginning there was a separate system of education for the sexes.

In New England girls were generally excluded from town schools, although a few districts did admit them. It was not until 1789 that Boston specifically provided for both sexes. The central colonies were more liberal, but even there girls attended "dame" or "common schools," never having access to the college preparatory "Latin grammar schools." While females could have a decent elementary education, and upper-class young ladies might attend "academies" in which they were taught such graces as French and embroidery, higher education was completely out of the question. The American forefathers set up along a far-flung frontier nine colleges before independence—and seven more during the years of a bloody war and the confusion of establishing a new country in the wake of a revolution— but the door of every single one was closed to women!

At first the schools reflected religious values, but when a number of religious sects began to demand greater freedom, paving the way for the separation of church and state, another cause emerged. America was a democracy. Unlike the Old World, where government was in the hands of the aristocracy, we required our schools to train citizens competent to govern *themselves*.

The Massachusetts School Act of 1642 specifically made provisions for "that learning which may be profitable to the Commonwealth." The duties of citizenship applied only to men, for women had no citizenship rights. In Colonial times women did not sit on local governing councils. After the Revolution, when legislatures, Federal and state and local, established American civil law, they followed the English common law—that is to say, that body of law that grew from custom and habit rather than from formal code. In the new country, as in old England, women could neither vote nor hold office, had no voice in the laws that were to govern the country, and indeed, they could not even sit on juries. More than that, while all women were disenfranchised, married women, as described by Sir William Blackstone in his outline of English common law, were "civilly dead." They could not sign wills or deeds, sue or be sued, own property, or testify in court.

The notion that women were inferior morally and unsuited to abstract thinking which would be useful for government or the professions became a self-fulfilling prophecy. Little boys could look forward to the possibility of going on to the colleges, which were primarily training for the ministry, or into scholarship in the classics. Little girls attended "dame schools" (often co-educational), which were taught by ministers' wives in their own homes. But they never were able to go beyond the basics of "reading, writing, and 'rithmetic" because they had no access to further education. Although some of the dame schools were taught by highly competent women—Benjamin Franklin was to speak admiringly of his teacher, Madam Sarah Knight—low expectations were set on little girls. The neatly embroidered samplers they made, on which they cross-stitched the letters of the alphabet and a line or two from the Bible, were proof that they were educated as women ought to be—in reading, writing, religion, and handiwork. To be able to read the Bible and perform the duties of caring for a home was sufficient for girls, their parents thought. An old diary written by her father proudly records Mary Sewell's fifth birthday on October 28, 1691, with this entry: "Mary goes to Mrs. Thair's to learn to Read and Knit."

The beginnings of change—new ideas that would challenge age-old beliefs about women's rights and capacities—did not come until the close of the eighteenth century. Then, both in America and abroad, there were stirrings of a new consciousness, started in part by the ideas of the American and French revolutions. The question inevitably arose: If "man" was endowed with certain natural and inalienable rights, why not *woman* as well? Even as the Revolutionary War raged, patriot Thomas Paine raised the issue in an essay published in the *Pennsylvania Magazine* in August 1775:

> even in countries where they may be esteemed the most happy, women are constrained in their desires in the disposal of their goods, robbed of freedom and will by the laws, the slaves of opinion. . . . Who does not feel for the tender sex?

The cudgels were soon taken up by a remarkable young Anglo-Irishwoman who was Tom Paine's friend. Mary Wollstonecraft went to France to witness the battles of the French Revolution, and wrote a tract called

55

A Vindication of the Rights of Man. In 1792 she took the next step. In her little pamphlet *Vindication of the Rights of Women*, she set forth the basic ideas on which the battle for women's equality has been based ever since:

Women, Mary Wollstonecraft wrote, must "bow to the authority of reason, instead of being the *modest* slaves of opinion." She insisted that women are equal to men, and therefore are entitled to the same political and personal treatment as men. On that reasoning she outlined a fourfold program: Women had *a right to the same education as men; the right to be governed by the same moral standards as men; the right to enjoy the same political advantages and obligations as men; the right to the same work opportunities as men.*

While Mary Wollstonecraft was outlining her program, economic forces here and abroad were adding weight to her arguments. In America Deborah Skinner took her place behind the first power loom in 1814. In a matter of only a few years, thousands of American women were summoned every morning by the shrill factory whistle that heralded the new industrial society. Finally, beyond the ideas spawned by the Revolution itself and the practical needs of a growing industrial economy, there was still another social force that would play its part in determining the place of women in America. That was the abolitionist movement, and its offshoot, the suffrage movement.

It was not only women who were victimized by the differences between the ideals of the American Revolution and the practices of the new nation. Despite the efforts of some of the founders of the new republic, the

Revolution did not outlaw slavery. In fact after 1793, when the cotton gin was invented, more workers were needed in the cotton fields, and slavery grew rapidly.

As slavery grew and became more profitable, conditions of slavery worsened. There were white people in America who came to see slavery as a dark side of American morality—they thought it had to be abolished. These dedicated abolitionists began to see that women were also oppressed and discriminated against. "We have good cause to be grateful to the slave," wrote the feminist and abolitionist Abby Kelley, a spirited Quaker, "for the benefit we have received to *ourselves*, in working for him. In striving to strike off his irons, we found, most surely, that *we* were manacled *ourselves*."

The abolitionist movement gave women their first cause and their first opportunity to come out of the obscurity of the home to take part in public debate. It was not an easy step. Angelina and Sarah Grimké, daughters of a South Carolina slaveholding family who moved to Philadelphia and became active abolitionists, found themselves the objects of derision for taking an "obtrusive . . . part in measures of reform," rather than working "modestly behind-the-scenes." Angelina's reply to criticism that she was "unfeminine" was characteristically gentle: "I recognize no rights but human rights, for in Jesus Christ there is neither male nor female." But to her close friends she raged: "What then can woman do for the slave when she herself is under the feet of man and shamed into silence?"

The same emotions motivated a Quaker abolitionist named Lucretia Mott and Elizabeth Cady Stanton, the young wife of an abolitionist leader. They had come to a

World Anti-Slavery Convention in the summer of 1840. The male delegates refused to seat women, and Mrs. Stanton and Mrs. Mott found themselves exiled to a park bench during meeting hours. There they spoke of their outrage at the position of women in America.

Mrs. Stanton explained her feelings this way:

> My experiences at the World Anti-Slavery Convention, all I had read of the legal status of women, and the oppression I see everywhere swept across my soul, intensified now by many personal experiences. It seemed as if all the elements had conspired to impel me to some onward step. I could not see what to do or where to begin—my only thought was a public meeting for protest and discussion.

It took eight years for the meeting to take place. In 1848 Mrs. Stanton and Mrs. Mott, with the help of three Quaker friends, took newspaper advertisements to "earnestly invite" women from neighboring towns to a "convention to discuss the social, civil and religious rights of women," in Seneca Falls, New York.

Over a hundred women signed the convention's Declaration of Principles—a manifesto that began, "We hold these truths to be self-evident; that all men and women are created equal." Then they set to work to secure their rights. Women, the delegates agreed, were entitled to property rights, which included *control of their own earnings*. They wanted *guardianship of their children*, in case of divorce. Most controversial of all the issues was the *right to the vote*. And underlying all the demands were the most basic of all: *Women had rights to educa-*

tion, to equality in the working world, and to the same aspirations as men.

The first women's movement set off a debate that would not be resolved until women got the vote in 1920, and would once again emerge in the 1960's to extend women's rights in all areas. But once it was launched, it was never again possible for public opinion to support the notion that *all* women were passive, content with second-class standing, uninterested in claiming all the rights and responsibilities that men had as a birthright.

Well before all the currents came together—the ideals of equality that came out of the American Revolution, the needs of the industrial society, the mobilization of women for the cause of abolition, which in turn led to the suffrage movement—foresighted American women were beginning to pave the way for their sisters' and daughters' admittance to higher education. In 1819 Emma Willard placed her pamphlet "An Address to the Public, Particularly to the Members of the Legislature of New York" in the hands of the state's governor, DeWitt Clinton.

Emma Willard's plan was the result of her own unusual educational experiments. As a little girl in Berlin, Connecticut, she was her father's favorite child; he delighted in giving her mathematical problems to solve and encouraging her lively intellectual curiosity. But then it all came to a dead end. When Mrs. Willard, by then the wife of a headmaster of a boys' academy and herself a teacher of girls, wrote to the University of Middlebury, in Vermont, for permission to take the entrance examinations, she was flatly turned down.

Emma Willard refused to be deterred. She taught herself algebra, geometry, and solid geometry. She had no textbooks, so she made pyramids and cones out of turnips and potatoes. "I spent from 10 to 12 hours a day in teaching . . . besides which having always under investigation some one new subject, which, as I studied, I simultaneously taught." Her students caught her fire, learned math, geography, history, and even the new "natural philosophy," as science was then called. Her friends encouraged her, telling her to outline her ideas in a pamphlet, with the hope of getting a charter and financial backing for a school of her own.

Luck was with Emma Willard. Foresighted Governor Clinton read her paper and gave her his support. So did the New York legislature, which she wooed by meeting quietly with one member after another. They gave her support but no funds to pay for the school whose charter they approved. Practical Mrs. Willard went across the Hudson River to industrial Troy and persuaded the town council to assign her four thousand dollars. In 1821, Troy Female Seminary, the first endowed school for girls, accepted its freshman class.

Women might be prepared for higher education, but what were they to do with that equipment? The likeliest starting point was Oberlin College, an institution that was founded by abolitionists in 1837. Oberlin declared that it was open to higher education for all—regardless of race or sex. But despite its promise to provide for "the elevation of the female character, bringing within the reach of the misjudged and the neglected sex all the instructive privileges which have unreasonably distinguished the leading sex from theirs," Oberlin offered women only a shortened "literary course." As Lucy Stone, a feminist who was one of the college's first graduates, wrote later,

> Oberlin's attitude was that women's high calling was to be the mothers of the race, and that they should stay within that special sphere in order that future generations should not suffer from the . . . want of mother care. . . . Washing the men's clothes, caring for their rooms, serving them at table, listening to their orations, but themselves remaining respectfully silent in public assemblages, the Oberlin co-eds were being prepared for intelligent motherhood and a properly subservient wifehood.

While the established institutions of higher education hedged on woman's role, there were women themselves to take the initiative. Such a woman was Catharine Beecher, born to a family that believed the sexes were equal, and that tutored at home both sons and daughters. Catharine's sisters and brothers were abolitionists, ministers, writers—one of her sisters, Harriet Beecher Stowe, was the author of *Uncle Tom's Cabin.* Catharine followed the family dedication to the intellect by conducting a successful seminary for girls in Hartford, Connecticut, from 1823 to 1827.

Catharine Beecher observed the direction that industrialization was taking. The men were going westward, following the frontier, she decided, while the East was full of "surplus" females, forced to earn their own livings in factories. The best hope women had, she reasoned, was to follow their own "biological" bent—either to become teachers, a woman's calling, or to capitalize on their needed domestic skills.

Catharine Beecher set out to develop her ideas through a series of books on domestic science, physical culture, and "marriage problems." Her major treatise, *The American Woman's Home*, is a step-by-step guide to cooking, cleaning house, sewing, and home planning "for comfort and health."

More important was her contribution to teacher training. Teaching had not yet come to be considered a profession. The majority of teachers were men, whose own educations might have included a smattering of the classics at best but no courses in methods of teaching. No better prepared were the women who instructed the youngest children. Correctly foreseeing the time when secondary education would be the norm throughout America, Catharine Beecher resolved to make teaching a true profession. She developed a plan for what came to be called "normal schools," to be located in the Midwest, the part of the country where she thought the future population was headed, and to be open only to women. In order to gain support for her ambitious proposals, she established two fund-raising organizations: The American Women's Educational Association, in 1852, and The National Board of Popular Education, in 1857. Eventually her efforts resulted in three schools—of which one, Milwaukee-Downer, still survives.

Mary Lyon took over where Catharine Beecher stopped. As headmistress of two successful "ladies' academies," she was dissatisfied with what passed for women's education. She had watched her friend Catharine

Beecher lose her health battling almost unconquerable odds. More than that, as she wrote, "during the past year my heart has so yearned over the adult female youth in the common walks of life that it has sometimes seemed as if there was a fire shut up in my bones." To her mother she confided, "I have for a great while been thinking about these young ladies who find it necessary to make such an effort for their education as I made when I was obtaining mine. . . . My heart has burned within me; and again, I have bid it be quiet."

In 1834 Mary decided she could no longer bank her fires. She had worked out a plan for a new kind of educational institution for women—a place of higher learning that offered no less than the colleges and universities that men attended. Mary Lyon's asset, besides her vision and dedication, was a real genius for sales promotion, and somehow she persuaded the influential businessmen of the community to back her to the tune of the twenty-seven thousand dollars it would take to open her school.

The plan soon fell into limbo, though. Her backers meant well, but the panic and depression of 1837 were a setback. The businessmen's pleas for donations met with resistance from people who needed their money for their own security in hard times. Mary Lyon was forced to take to the road herself, carrying a green velvet traveling bag which became her trademark, arranging meetings in public halls and private houses, to raise the funds the school would need.

Miss Lyon's letters and diaries give a vivid picture of her society's view of woman's place. "What do I do that is wrong?" she asked indignantly.

> I ride in the stage-coach . . . without an escort.
> Other ladies do the same. I visit a family where I
> have been previously invited, and the minister's
> wife or some leading woman calls the ladies to-
> gether to see me, and I lay our object before them.
> . . . What harm is in that? . . . My heart is pained
> with the empty gentility, this genteel nothingness. I
> am doing a great work. . . . I cannot come down.

Mary Lyon's "great work" took form as Mount
Holyoke—the first college for women in America. Unwilling to wait until dormitory space was constructed,
Miss Lyon opened the doors to the partially built main
hall in November 1837, with the promise from towns-
women of South Hadley, Massachusetts, that they would
temporarily house the students in guest rooms, cots in
attics, and even haylofts.

Mount Holyoke remains an important institution of
higher learning to this day. More than that, it has served
as a model for the other women's colleges that were to
follow. There was Vassar, founded in Poughkeepsie,
New York, by Matthew Vassar, who wanted "to build
and endow a college for young women which shall be
to them what Yale and Harvard are to young men."

The college was incorporated as "Vassar Female
College." It was a title that sat badly with one of
Matthew Vassar's friends, the ardent feminist Sarah J.
Hale, who was editor of *Godey's Lady's Book*, the first
American "women's magazine." Mrs. Hale asked the
philanthropist to reconsider the name. If, indeed, the col-
lege he proposed was to be based on the belief that there

were no differences between the intellectual capacities and needs of men and women, why make the distinction "female?" "What 'female' do you mean?" she wrote tartly to him. "Not a female donkey?" Matthew Vassar was amused and persuaded. He changed the name, and subsequent colleges for women—Smith and Wellesley in 1875, the "Harvard Annex" of 1879 (later to be renamed Radcliffe College), and Bryn Mawr in 1885—were simply designated as "colleges."

The long struggle for equal educational opportunities for women which began with institutions that were "separate but equal" gradually expanded to include coeducation—the education of men and women in the same schools. Oberlin's admission of women to college classes in 1837—"the gray dawn of our morning," as Lucy Stone described it—paved the way for other colleges. Hillsdale College, in Michigan, gave its first A.B. degree to a woman in 1852. Albion College, also in Michigan, and Ohio's Antioch College, as well as another handful of colleges and universities in the Midwest, all were coeducational before the Civil War. The state universities, again led by those in the Midwest, followed the example of private colleges. The State University of Iowa granted a bachelor's degree to a woman in 1863; all departments were declared open to women at the University of Wisconsin by 1866.

The thrust toward higher education for women came from the stubborn courage of a handful of exceptional women. The admission of girls into the secondary-school system, on an equal basis with boys, sprang more directly from changes in nineteenth-century American society.

The waves of immigration that flooded the factories with foreign labor, beginning with the Irish potato famine in 1846, made America a country of many tongues and diverse cultures. Children had to be taught a new language, and they had to learn American values if they were to take their places as citizens. Then, too, the rise of technology required more and more education. Simple reading and writing and arithmetic were more than enough equipment to run a hand loom. To read a blueprint, keep business records, and eventually operate machinery such as typewriters and calculating machines, a worker had to have something beyond a basic education. To achieve those goals, the United States had to turn away from private systems of education based on economic class and national and religious distinctions, and open a system of secondary schools that would be free, publicly supported, and publicly controlled.

Once again, Massachusetts led the way. Compulsory education became the law there in 1852, and by 1918 every state required boys and girls to attend school until at least the age of sixteen. From the beginning high schools were open to girls as well as boys, and it soon became apparent that educators would have less difficulty persuading parents of daughters that school attendance was necessary. Boys were more likely than girls to be sent to work to bring home earnings for the family, for they earned so much more. As a result, every year since the Civil War has seen more girls than boys graduate from high school.

The remarkable progress of women into secondary and higher education between the American Revolution and the Civil War is so inspiring it is easy to miss the broken rung in the ladder. The hard-won benefits of education were gained only by *white* women. For their black sisters, the doors to equal education refused to budge.

In the South, where there was slavery, all blacks were deliberately kept illiterate—it was illegal to teach blacks to read. But even in the "free North" there were heavy obstacles for black girls looking for an education. If a white woman was less capable mentally than a man, and if all blacks were inferior to whites—the prevailing view except in the most advanced circles—then it followed that black girls were the least educable of all. Since it was considered a "lack of propriety" at the very least to try to educate a black young woman, there were few opportunities for the myths to be destroyed.

Prudence Crandall, a Quaker who conducted a successful school for young ladies in Canterbury, Connecticut, challenged the stereotype. Her servant, a free black woman, persuaded Miss Crandall to accept a black girl named Sarah Harris as a student in 1833. The "outraged" neighborhood demanded that she oust her pupil. Miss Crandall closed her school instead.

Undaunted, Prudence Crandall, like Mary Lyon, took to the road to gain support for her cause. She traveled to Boston, Providence, and New York to seek the advice of abolitionist leaders. She advertised in *The Liberator*, an antislavery newspaper, asking black parents to send their daughters to her for instruction. Two months after she closed her first school, she opened another—this time with *seventeen* young black women!

The city fathers tried every method to deter the

schoolmistress and her pupils. They took legal means, rushing a bill through the Connecticut legislature making it illegal for a Connecticut citizen to teach a pupil from another state. While this measure dragged through the courts, the townspeople resorted to hooliganism. The school's windows were broken, stones were thrown at pupils and teachers, manure was dropped in the well. Finally, after an arson attempt had gutted the cellar, masked men using battering rams demolished the first floor of the house while the women took refuge on the floor above. Fearful for the lives of her charges, Prudence Crandall conceded defeat and closed the school.

During the next twenty years there was little progress in the battle for the education of black women. When the next step was taken—the opening of the first school to train black women as teachers, in Washington, D.C., in 1851—it launched a battle as fierce as that around Prudence Crandall's school.

The founder of the school that was to bear her name, Myrtilla Miner was a poor girl from a village in central New York. In desperation because no higher education was available to her, she even wrote to the governor of the state, William H. Seward, asking for advice. He told her patronizingly that he hoped things would be better for her—but offered no other aid. Eventually she was admitted to a Quaker seminary in Rochester, New York.

As a white northerner, Myrtilla knew little about slavery. But after she graduated from the seminary, she became a teacher in a school for planters' daughters in Mississippi, and there she saw the plight of black slaves. Her request—to teach the slaves' children on her own time—was denied. Deeply stirred, she returned to the

North to consult with antislavery leaders about her plan to open a school for black girls on the level of a "first class school of the other sex."

The place Miss Miner chose was Washington, D.C., because its laws permitted the education of "free colored children." She consulted with abolitionist leaders. They warned her that her plan was dangerous. "In my fancy I saw this little woman harassed by the law," wrote the great abolitionist Frederick Douglass, himself an escaped slave, "insulted in the street, the victim of slave-holding malice, and possibly, beaten down by the mob." Despite Douglass' well-founded fears, she solicited contributions from the leaders of the antislavery movement and the Quakers in Philadelphia and New York. Harriet Beecher Stowe gave her one thousand dollars from her royalties on *Uncle Tom's Cabin*; the most respected educators of the day, Horace Mann, Catharine Beecher, and others, were on her board of trustees. Miss Miner opened her school in the autumn of 1851 with six pupils. Within a month there were forty students.

Frederick Douglass' fears were soon justified. From time to time there were outbreaks of serious vandalism. Several times the school had to be moved. "At one o'clock I was awoke by the smoke of cracking fire," Myrtilla Miner wrote later, describing the worst episode.

> I opened the door from my chamber directly into the next, and . . . then hurriedly threw on a dress, rushed to the front chamber window and cried fire! fire! with awful fury—then with a pail I ran for water . . . then the neighbors came, and one going onto the roof soon allayed the fire, but when I got

back into our room the fire had entered there. . . . For years I had been expecting this so it did not take me unawares, but for the last year the ruffians had been so quiet I tho't they had given me up.

It was Myrtilla Miner who refused to give up. She cornered congressmen, journalists, newspaper publishers for aid. By 1857 she had built an institution with three departments—primary teaching, home economy, teacher training. Although its founder's ill health forced the school to close in 1859 (she died in 1864), and it was not reopened for some years, Miner Teachers College sent its graduates out to teach all over the country until 1955. It still exists today, as part of the integrated District school system, under the name District of Columbia Teachers College.

Miner Teachers College temporarily stopped operations during the Civil War along with a number of other educational institutions. For that matter, women's struggles to advance in work, education, and citizenship rights all ground to a halt. The nation plunged into a bloody war over the issue of slavery and the most important question of all—whether or not the Union was to survive. Women would have to wait for calmer times before they could once again take up their own cause.

5

The Civil War and Its Aftermath

In November 1862 a tall, spare New Englander recorded a dramatic decision in her diary. "Thirty years old," Louisa May Alcott wrote. "Decided to go to Washington as a nurse if I could find a place." And then, in December,

> I started on my long journey . . . into a new world full of stirring sights and sounds, new adventures, and an ever-growing sense of the great task I had undertaken. I said my prayers as I went rushing through the country white with tents, all alive with patriotism, and already red with blood.

The War Between the States had been brewing for years before the guns of Fort Sumter sounded its beginning on April 12, 1861. Behind the immediate cause—conflict over the issue of extending slavery into the new territories—were economic reasons. Since the beginning of the eighteenth century the North had moved at an ever increasing rate toward industrialization, in which workers labored for wages, while the South remained largely agrarian, and people took their living from the soil. These differences put the sections of the country into battle over such matters as tariffs and westward expansion. By the 1860's industrialization had grown at such a rate that the interests of North and South were bound to come into head-on collision.

In the North, homecrafts belonged to the past. Power looms replaced handweaving as five million power-driven spindles bobbed to turn out millions of yards of factory-made fabric. Northern industrial output reached an undreamed-of total worth of nearly two billion dollars in the year before the war. To provide the labor needed for industries—textiles, clothing, shoes, cigar making, paper manufacture, printing—required a workforce of well over a million, of whom more than one in four was a woman.

In the South the burden of production was on the four million black slaves who worked the land. The South's raw material, cotton, was shipped North and to England. There were virtually no factories, no large groups of women who earned a living in manufacturing or processing. The Southern white woman earned no wages, and saw herself protected by her "menfolks," even though her labor contributed to the work of a family enterprise.

The Civil War thrust Southern as well as Northern women into the workforce. Four million American men, Confederate and Union soldiers, were called into service. Women had to earn the money to support fatherless families, not only do their own work but take over the chores that men had shared. They spun cloth and sewed it for soldiers' uniforms, plowed, sowed, hoed, and reaped the crops needed to feed the families at home and the armies.

Anna Shaw, a suffrage leader and orator, describes the years of the war in a memoir of her girlhood:

> The problem of living grew harder with every day. We eked out our little income in every way we could, taking boarders . . . making quilts, which we sold. Again my mother did such outside sewing as she could secure, yet with every month . . . the gulf between our income and our expenses grew wider, and the price of the bare necessities of existence climbed up and up. The largest amount I could earn at teaching was six dollars a week. . . . It was an incessant struggle to keep our land, pay our taxes, and to live. . . . There were no men left to grind our corn, to get in our crops, or to care for our livestock; and all around us we saw our struggle reflected in the lives of our neighbors.

Most of all, women worked to save lives. Like Louisa May Alcott, some two thousand other women from the North and South were willing to risk their health and even their lives to nurse the wounded in hospitals and on the battlefield.

Historically, nursing has been considered "women's work." The role of an "angel of mercy" who relieved the suffering of the stricken was close to that of a mother, who cared for helpless children. Such early "hospitals" as the Hôtel Dieu, founded in Paris in the seventh century, and St. Thomas's and St. Bartholomew's hospitals in London were staffed by women volunteers. There were nuns in a number of religious orders whose task it was to bring food and water to the ill, to bathe them, to offer loving care and solace. Principles of hygiene and modern medicine were unknown until the nineteenth century, and nursing was a job that required a kindly heart, not education or intellect.

In America, too, nursing was a lowly occupation. The first secular hospital was established on Manhattan Island by the Dutch West India Company in 1658 as a pesthouse—a place where the sick were simply quarantined, in order to reduce the chance of contagion. It later became a combination city poorhouse, house of correction and penitentiary, orphan asylum for the pauper sick and insane. Much later it became New York's famous Bellevue Hospital. Old Blockley, founded in 1713, later to become Philadelphia General Hospital, had a similar history and characteristics—squalor, filth, high death rate, an indifferent medical staff. Although the nurses there were paid, they were untrained and classed as "domestics."

The first attempts to make nursing a profession were the work of Valentine Seaman, a physician at the New York Hospital, who developed a course of twenty-four lectures for nurses in 1798. But Dr. Seaman's ideas did not spread. When Dr. Elizabeth Blackwell, the first woman physician in America, opened the New York Infirmary, the first hospital entirely staffed by women, she found that her nurses had little more than good instincts to guide them in caring for the sick. Courageous Dr. Blackwell turned toward her friend Florence Nightingale, a British aristocrat who has come to be viewed as the founder of modern nursing and public health care. Using Florence Nightingale's theories, Dr. Blackwell set up a small nurses' training school in New York in 1858.

A few hundred trained nurses could hardly make a dent in the enormous problem of caring for the hundreds of thousands of Civil War casualties. Women volunteers in New York City rushed in to fill the gap. They hastily set up an organization, the Women's Central Association of Relief, which later became the U.S. Sanitary Commission. They organized volunteer groups and gave the women a short, intensive training course on the care of the sick and injured. More important, they sent urgent bulletins to government and other agencies pleading for the establishment of a nursing corps. Over the objections of the Army Medical Corps, the Union government in 1861 appointed Dorothea Dix—well known for her pioneering work in reforming prisons and insane asylums—to head the nursing service in the Union Army hospitals.

The Sanitary Commission itself was headed by men: Dr. Henry Bellows, a Unitarian minister, was its president, and the brilliant landscape architect Frederick Law Olmsted served as its secretary-general. But the money was raised by thousands of women volunteers. In the field itself it was women who carried on the exhausting, often dangerous job of tending the casualties.

The Sanitary Commission became the backbone of the Union hospital and medical services. It recruited the nurses for army hospital services, dealing directly with Dorothea Dix. The staunch old reformer ran a tight ship: Nurses were required to be "over thirty, plain, and strong enough to turn a man over in bed"—as well as to do the dirtiest and hardest work. In spite of the stringent regulations, there was no shortage of recruits. Answering to the greeting "Hello Sanitary," dedicated women moved among the rows of cots, bringing food, clean clothing, soap, and sometimes small gifts to the wounded men.

The medical volunteers had to work against heavy handicaps. Provisions were often scarce; there were shortages of food, bandages, medicine. The soldiers' diet was inadequate, and scurvy was rampant. The women worked prodigiously. They agitated for better sanitation in the army camps. They banded together into more than seven thousand local societies throughout the North and West, and raised the fifty million dollars needed to maintain hospital ships, relief camps, and convalescent homes.

Some of the volunteers worked in the battlefields, often in range of gunfire and cannonballs. Among them was Clara Barton, a schoolteacher from Massachusetts. Shortly before the war began Miss Barton moved to Washington, D.C., to take a job as a clerk in the U.S. Patent Office. There, close to the seat of the government, she watched the Union gear up for war. It didn't take her long to decide what part she would play during the emergency. At the outbreak she acted on her own initiative to obtain and distribute supplies for the relief of wounded soldiers.

Clara Barton's work took her to the bloodiest battlefields—Antietam and Chancellorsville among them. A young black woman, Susie King Taylor, who nursed convalescents at Sea Island, Georgia, observed her solicitude for the black soldiers, who served in segregated regiments. "I honored her," wrote Mrs. Taylor, "for her devotion and care of these men."

Even after the signing of the peace in 1865, Clara Barton's work did not end. There remained the tracing of missing soldiers. In answer to the heartbroken pleas of families who knew only that their men had not come home, she organized a bureau of records to aid in the search. It was not for another four years that Clara Barton finally ended her war vigil and went abroad for a rest.

The holiday was not to last long. In 1870 the Franco-Prussian war broke out in Europe, and Clara Barton again plunged into the task of aiding the victims of war. This time she found an organization already established to provide relief. It was the International Red Cross, a society that had been founded in 1863 in Geneva, Switzerland, when delegates from fourteen countries agreed to commit their governments to provide medical and emergency aid to wounded soldiers, whether enemy or friend, in time of war. With clear memories of the horrors of the Civil War—the wounded and dying men agonizing in the pain of gangrene from untreated injuries, the plagues of dysentery, pneumonia, and the other diseases brought on by lack of care and facilities—she returned to America in 1873 to begin her campaign to bring her country into the Geneva Convention.

Clara Barton's hopes were realized when the United States became a signatory to the convention in 1882. The tireless nurse embarked on what she considered her most important work—a career that lasted some twenty years. She became the first president of the American Red Cross. In the years she headed the organization—she held the post until 1904—Clara Barton increased the organization's scope. It was not only in time of war that suffering people needed relief, she decided. She framed the "American" amendment to the constitution of the Red Cross, providing for aid in times of famine, flood, earthquake, and plague.

While Clara Barton was in Europe envisioning the care of the sick on an international scale, American women were reforming the nursing profession at home. The Civil War had brought more than six hundred thousand battlefield casualties, and attention had been drawn to the sorry condition of nursing. It had also given experience to women like Louisa Lee Schuyler, a volunteer in the Sanitary Commission, who, like Clara Barton, resolved to continue her mission after the war.

Louisa Schuyler decided that the first step was to make the public aware of what health care was really like. Under the auspices of the New York State Charities Aid Association—a volunteer group in which she was active—she organized visitors' teams to Bellevue Hospital. The horrified observers saw patients dying in their own filth, while the "nurses," who were drawn from the underworld of vagrancy and workhouse poverty, terrorized the sick, accepted fees and bribes, stole the medicine they were supposed to be dispensing, and even neglected to bring food to the invalids.

The tour did the trick. In England Florence Nightingale had already published an immense volume of notes on health conditions in the British army that outlined a course on sanitation, diet, and treatment of the sick in accord with principles of modern medicine. She had also pioneered the first training school for nurses in England at St. Thomas's hospital in London. The reformers studied Nightingale's methods and moved to establish American schools of nursing.

Three schools were opened, one at Bellevue and the others in Boston and New Haven. Although the schools were connected with hospitals, they were independent, and each was headed by a nurse—a female—not a doctor. Reaction was swift and angry. Physicians and the general public were outraged: It was one thing for nurses to work under a physician's direction, but quite another for them to seek professional standing! Nevertheless, the women refused to back down. Eventually the plan's opponents were won over by the excellent nursing care given by the students and graduates of the school.

With the ground broken, nursing rapidly advanced in the next fifty years. A conference on hospitals, dispensaries, and nursing at the Chicago World's Fair in 1893 led to the formation of the first national organization of nurses. Originally named the American Society of Superintendents of Training Schools for Nurses, it became the National League of Nursing Education in 1912. By 1925 there were more than 2,500 schools turning out trained nurses, as well as other organizations whose goal was to improve the quality of nursing in America. In 1903, North Carolina responded from pressure within the profession by setting requirements for state examination and registration of nurses; within the next twenty years, every state had such laws. Working against the odds of prejudice and indifference, women in the nursing field won the right to training and dignity in their work. They changed the care of the sick from a haphazard "mission of duty" to a respected profession that today employs well over a half million women.

The professionalizing of nursing, important as it was, was still only one by-product of the Civil War. The conflict and its aftermath brought women into vocational areas that had never been opened to them before, and in never-before-imagined numbers.

The Civil War opened government service to women. More than four hundred women fought side by side with uniformed soldiers in the Union Army, and one of them—Dr. Mary Walker, a physician who practiced in a man's swallow-tailed coat—won the Congressional Medal of Honor. More significantly, the war brought women into the offices that administered the Federal government and established them for the first time as white-collar workers.

Before the war, a workforce of men operated the clerical level in government. When men went to the front, women were recruited to fill in as clerks and bookkeepers. Hordes of women arrived in Washington, some seeking work for patriotic reasons—a wish to support the Union and hasten an end to the war—and others because their wages were needed to support families with no male breadwinners. The first Civil Service Act, which made government jobs available on the basis of merit rather than on a politician's personal preference, was not passed until 1883; until then there were no formal job qualifications, and any applicant might be considered for any position. Women were able to prove their competence to fill government positions during the Civil War, and once they had gained entry, never relinquished it.

The Civil War was the turning point for women in the teaching profession, too. While women had slowly moved into teaching during the first part of the nineteenth century, they had many obstacles to overcome in breaking down the prejudice that said they lacked the necessary mentality. The shortage of men during the Civil War and the growing press for mass education demanded that they be recruited to teach. Within a few years after the end of the war, public opinion grew to accept teaching as a female occupation.

Finally, the end of the Civil War brought a resurgence to the cause of women's rights. The suffrage movement had gone dormant during the conflict, for given a choice between working for their own interests or for the principle of freeing the slaves, women opted for putting their efforts into emancipation. They hoped that when peace came, and the freed slaves were given citizenship, the franchise and other rights would be extended to include women, too.

Elizabeth Cady Stanton, one of the founders of the suffrage movement, and her close associate, Susan B. Anthony, a former schoolteacher who devoted her life to women's rights, sent out a call to women all over the country to join them at a meeting of "The Loyal Women of the Nation" in New York City on May 13, 1863. "At this hour the best word and work of every man and woman are imperatively demanded," the summons read.

> To man . . . is assigned the forum, the camp and field. What is woman's legitimate work and how she may best accomplish it, is worthy our earnest counsel. . . . Woman is equally interested and responsible . . . in the settlement of this final problem of

self-government; therefore let none stand idle spectators now.

Hundreds of women responded to the call. They pledged their support to collect a million signatures to a petition asking Congress to emancipate the slaves. A stream of letters went out all across the nation, as far away as California. On February 9, 1864, two tall black men—symbolic figures—actually delivered enormous bundles made up of petition rolls into the Senate Chamber and placed them on the desk of Charles Sumner, the Senator from Massachusetts.

The fruits of the women's hard work on behalf of the Union and abolition were bitter. The war's end brought no advances in women's rights. The Republicans, whom the feminists had backed, anticipated two million new male black voters once former slaves had the franchise. Certain that they were to become the majority party, they were unwilling to jeopardize their gains by agitating for the unpopular cause of women's rights. The Fourteenth Amendment, in fact, which prevented the States from denying former slaves their citizenship rights, actually introduced the word "male" into the Constitution for the first time. Now there was a real question about whether women were even citizens of the United States!

Women's disappointment about being passed over for the vote, after years of devoted work for abolition and for a Union victory, was one reason that the suffrage movement sprang once again to life after the war's end. A second reason was that the war had wrought changes in the lives of so many American women. Most of the women who went to work during the war emergency remained part of a permanent workforce. There was an increasingly large new group of women in the two professions of teaching and nursing. Colleges and universities were opening to women, and for the first time there was a sizeable number of educated women. The presence of women in government offices meant that they had cracked the all-male white-collar world. In short, women could take on the responsibility of earning a living—but they could not control their own money. They could support children, but had no custody rights. They could file and keep books in government offices—have a part in the actual administration of government—but they could not vote. Women's civil rights simply had not kept pace with vocational change, and it was apparent that something had to be done!

There were two schools of thought about how women were to accomplish their ends. One group, headed by Elizabeth Cady Stanton and Susan B. Anthony, believed that women needed a separate Amendment to the Constitution guaranteeing them the right to vote. Other activists disagreed; they thought the most promising area was through state and local legislation. The Stanton-Anthony alliance founded the all-woman National Woman Suffrage Organization, while Lucy Stone became head of the American Woman Suffrage Association, made up primarily of former abolitionists. Once organized, the two groups set about seeking their common cause through widely different methods—and often they were at swords' points.

Although suffragists were divided about how women were to secure their rights, there was no disagreement on the question of working women's needs for equal jobs and equal pay. Feminists directed themselves to answering the arguments that were used to keep women in lower paying work—the very same excuses that justified denying women their civil rights. Women, went the myth, needed special protection—they were the "weaker sex." No one spoke more eloquently against that stereotype than Sojourner Truth, a freed black slave who became a spokeswoman for both abolition and women's rights.

Sojourner Truth chose her name for its symbolism, for she saw herself as a traveler in search of God's truth, which she thought was the equality of all people—black and white, male and female. Her legal name was Isabella Van Wagener, given to her by the last of her masters, who bought her and set her free after her previous master had kept her on a pretext when New York abolished slavery in 1827. Like other slaves she never was allowed to learn to read or write, but as she later told audiences who came to hear her from the Atlantic to the Western frontier: "Children, I talk to God and God talks to me!" God and the law remained her guides: Her first free act was a court battle in which she recovered her little boy, sold illegally into the South.

Sojourner Truth's travels as a speaker in the abolitionist cause took her to a Utopian commune in Northampton, Massachusetts. There she saw, for the first time, men and women living and working on an equal basis. She became convinced that the cause of women's rights was as important as antislavery. Her own life had required too much strength and courage—she had survived one abusive master after another—for her to accept the

An Exxon paleontologist works at an offshore oil site.

An employee at Exxon's East Texas oil fields helps lay a pipeline.

An eighteenth-century engraving depicts a soap-and-candle merchant, employment typical of many colonial women.

In colonial days, as today, printing and bookmaking employed many women, and while there were a few who printed their own newspapers, many found themselves relegated to womanly tasks such as sewing, pictured above.

Woman as "schoolmarm." Above, during colonial times in a one-room schoolhouse; below, in a freedmen's school in Vicksburg, Mississippi.

St. Luke's Hospital operating room, 1899.

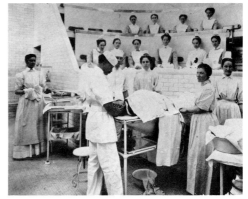

Civil War nurse

As a helping job, nursing has always been, and remains today, mainly women's work. These photographs reflect the movement nurses have made from "angels of mercy" to professional medical personnel.

A clinic in a New York City hospital, c. 1914.

The Chrisman sisters homesteaded in this Nebraska sod house.

Going West often meant leaving behind the narrow attitudes of the East and entering a world where women had the opportunity to follow their own inclinations.

"Calico Queens of the honkytonks" celebrate the end of the trail with the cowboys.

The Working Women's Protective Union interviewing applicants in its female employment agency. 1879 woodcut.

idea that women were frail. Listen to her answer to a clergyman at a suffrage meeting in Akron, Ohio, when he insisted that women were too "delicate" to vote:

"The man over there says women need to be helped into carriages and lifted over ditches," Sojourner Truth began softly. "Nobody helps me into carriages or over puddles . . . and ain't I a woman?" Her voice rising, she thrust out her bare arm.

> Look at my arm! I have ploughed and planted—and no man could head me—and ain't I a woman? I could work as much and eat as much as a man—when I could get it—and hear the lash as well! And ain't I a woman? I have borne thirteen children and seen most of them sold into slavery, and when I cried out with my mother's grief, none but Jesus heard me—and ain't I a woman?

Susan B. Anthony, too, used her short-lived but militant newspaper, *The Revolution*, to dispel the canards that told women they were too fragile for "men's work." "A steam sawmill in Bristol, Indiana, is managed by a man and his two daughters," an article in the January 22, 1868, issue proclaims. "One of the girls is engineer and fireman, and the other helps her father lift the boards and roll the logs."

Suffragists gave aid and encouragement to working women in more direct ways, too. In 1868, the following notice appeared in *The Revolution*:

> A meeting of ladies was held on September 17 at noon, in the offices of *The Revolution* newspaper for the purpose of organizing an association of

working women which might act for the interest of its members, in the same manner as the associations of workingmen now regulate the wages, etc., of those belonging to them.

The meeting was a success. It not only sprouted the Women's Typographical Union, under the leadership of a skilled typesetter named Augusta Lewis, but it also joined two previously separate movements—that of women's citizenship rights and the cause of the working woman. Hardworking Susan B. Anthony cheered the unionists: "Girls," she wrote, "you must take this matter to heart seriously, for you are placed, and by your own efforts, on a level with men . . . to obtain wages for your labor. . . . You have taken a great, a momentous step forward in the path to success." Then she went on to press, through the union, for a chance to present the cause of suffrage to the public.

One of the few men of his time who saw the connection between the two movements was the National Labor Union's William Sylvis. In 1868 he invited Elizabeth Cady Stanton and Susan B. Anthony to address a meeting.

The two suffragists created a sensation. Although the *New York Herald* found Miss Anthony "delightfully insinuating," and wrote that she "made no mean impression on the bearded delegates," the male delegates were outraged. They refused to endorse her "peculiar ideas," for while they were willing to concede, along with Sylvis, that women "deserve equal pay for equal work . . . it is only just and humane," the suffragists' insistence that women also be allowed to vote was going entirely too far.

But whether the "bearded delegates" were ready or not, both equal pay and equal rights, as well as the suffragists' "peculiar" theories about citizenship, were ideas whose time had come. While the debates about suffrage and women's parity on the labor market were to continue in the East until well into the twentieth century, less than a year after Miss Anthony and Mrs. Stanton took the podium in New York, quietly and without fanfare the Territory of Wyoming passed the first "equal pay for equal work" law and at the same time gave women the vote. The tide had turned—at least on the frontier!

6

On the Frontier

It seems only natural that the first real gains for women in their struggle for job equality and civil rights took place on the Western frontier. From the beginning, pioneer women were an integral part of the westward expansion that moved the frontier of America from the Hudson River to the Pacific Coast. Overcoming the natural hazards of an inhospitable territory—first Ohio, then Illinois, Kansas, Texas, the Dakotas, and finally across the Great Divide and on out to the West Coast—required all the courage and resources that both men and women possessed. The land was there for the asking; homesteaders merely had to mark off territory with stakes and string to own it. But to survive the long, cold winters, families had to be able to keep warm, have enough to eat, provide the basic necessities of life.

John Ise describes women's work in *Sod and Stubble*, the biography of his mother, one of the German immigrants who pioneered Kansas. Mrs. Ise helped to build the sod house—a shelter made of strips of earth and fiber, with a thatched roof made of young willow trees. She worked side by side with her husband, planting, harvesting, fighting the grasshoppers that descended like a biblical plague to eat the grain and the prairie fires that swept across the summer-dried land. Later, as the farm prospered and her sons grew up, Mrs. Ise, like other women on the prairie, saw the heavy field work taken over by men—hired hands and neighbors who would exchange services—while she processed and cooked food, made clothing, kept house.

Even without working in the fields, there was plenty for women to do. They tended kitchen gardens, where food was grown for the family's own use; helped with the livestock, pigs, and poultry; milked cows; churned butter. Women made their own household furnishings: brooms, mattresses, and floor mats from straw and corn husks; soap from lye and tallow; vinegar from molasses, rainwater, and yeast; and "coffee" from browned rye grain.

The frontier woman was, indeed, a special breed. She proved her ability to uphold her end of the load even where physical endurance was required. She bore the children, cared for them when they were sick, and often taught them to read and cipher. She tended her garden, cooked the family's food, and preserved what she could for the winter. And when danger from wild beasts threatened, she proved herself capable in the use of a gun.

Some of the women recorded their lives in letters and diaries. Recently a Radcliffe student named Joanna L. Stratton, visiting her grandmother in Topeka, Kansas, found a file cabinet in the attic. Inside there were manuscripts written by Kansas pioneer women which her grandmother had hoped to compile into a book. The nearly eight hundred personal memoirs of postmistresses and women preachers, mayors, teachers, and farmhands who grew up while the West was being won—in the days when covered wagons, stagecoach rides, and Indian raids were common—convey a vivid picture of frontier life.

There was Anna Morgan, for one. Her diary tells about her kidnapping by Indians a month after she was married. At first she was put to the hardest tasks; she had to "carry water and wood for the more favored squaws," she wrote. But perhaps life among the Indians was not so hard as being a frontierswoman, for after Colonel George A. Custer and the Seventh Cavalry helped rescue her and sent her home, Mrs. Morgan's diary records: "After I came back the road seemed rough, and I often wished they had never found me."

Another of the all-but-anonymous heroines was Emma Adair Remington—a niece of abolitionist John Brown. As a child on the "middle frontier" before the Civil War, she witnessed the bloody battle between abolitionist and proslavery forces at Osawatomic, Kansas, and her diary provides terrifying insights into the fierce struggle. An equally bloodcurdling story is told by Emaline M. Thompson, who settled with her husband on the Oregon Trail. Mrs. Thompson's adventurous life included a stint as innkeeper; the log cabin she built and expanded became well known along the route to California. Part of Mrs. Thompson's job was sharpshooting, for the mountains were the domain of wild animals that had not learned to keep their distance from civilization.

Looking back into old records, diaries, letters that

describe the harsh life of the frontier inevitably leads to this question: Why were so many women willing to leave the safety and security of settled communities to become part of the two great migrations that followed the War of 1812—the first across the lower South along the Gulf of Mexico, then up the Mississippi and the Red River to the Great Lakes as far as Michigan and Wisconsin; the second the push all the way out to the Pacific Coast? Some of the answer was in the women's own characters—their spirit of adventure, their need for independence and self-reliance. Mostly there were economic reasons, for after each period of recession in industry, the waves of westward migration increased. The government, anxious to see the West settled, encouraged migration by building roads and offering homestead privileges.

One way women were lured west was by such legislation as the Oregon Land Donation Act of 1850, which gave a man and wife 640 acres—a single woman or man 320 acres. Unlike in the East, where married women had no property rights, a wife in the Oregon Territory could own land. Single women, too, were encouraged to become farmers and ranchers. Even in country where men outnumbered women by four to one, an observer wrote, "The prairies were dotted with shacks on which women live and farm alone."

The Homestead Act in 1862 was a further impetus to westward migration. In the East waves of immigration, chiefly from Ireland, had flooded the industrial market with excess workers. Labor parties, newly formed to represent working people, saw westward expansion as a means of siphoning off the surplus labor that was driving wages down, and brought pressure on the government to offer land in the West on attractive enough terms to encourage families to move from the crowded cities into the wide-open frontier.

The Homestead Act provided that any citizen, or alien who wished to become a citizen, could file a claim for as many as 160 acres of "public-domain" land. The terms specified that the claimant had to either "cultivate or reside on" the acreage for at least five years—after which time permanent ownership was automatically granted. The law itself, attractive as it sounded, turned out to be a mixed blessing at best; most of the fertile land was already in private hands; there was no offer of training, nor any way in which day laborers or tenants could even acquire the money they needed to invest in housing materials, tools, fences, and livestock. Besides, there were loopholes in the law that eventually delivered desirable land to owners of huge estates. But all the drawbacks were not immediately apparent, and the passage of the bill brought men and women by the thousands to the plains and prairies to homestead.

Another draw for young women to go west was the railroad. Gold in Sutter's Mill in February 1849 began the gold rush to San Francisco. The hordes of prospectors, and then traders, merchants, builders, and engineers, who went in search of fortune hastened the completion of the first transcontinental railroad. By 1880 the legendary Santa Fe Trail from Independence, Missouri, to Santa Fe, New Mexico—which brought gold and silver, furs, skins, and wool from the territories eastward, and manufactured goods and other necessities west to the frontier—was paralleled with railroad tracks. Passage west became safe, comfortable, and reliable.

The railroad itself opened work for women. Although men were train engineers, firemen, porters, and conductors, the towns that grew up around the stations became small commercial centers which provided opportunities for women. Passengers on the railroad had to be fed along the way, and an enterprising restaurateur began the Harvey chain—the first "fast-food" operation. Hundreds of young women eagerly competed for the relatively highly paid jobs. Sleeping in dormitories, rising at dawn to dress in their pert uniforms, serving platters of flapjacks, fried potatoes, and fried chicken, and pitchers of steaming coffee, the young women plunged into their jobs with the sense of adventure that spurred a future generation of women to find work with the airlines.

Then, too, there was another group of women—colorful, hard living—who saw a chance to make quick fortunes by bringing escape from dreary solitude to miners, woodsmen, gold prospectors. What the men longed for was entertainment on their trips to frontier villages— the comradeship of women, the excitement of sex, the lusty pleasures of liquor, music, dancing. Saloonkeepers and barmaids, prostitutes and madams, cancan dancers and bar girls—the history of these women is preserved in legend and folktale, and in fictionalized accounts such as this one in Edna Ferber's novel of the Northwest, *Come and Get It*:

> When the girls at Sid LeMaire's Alcazar Theatre sold you beer it cost you a dollar a bottle. But it was worth it. . . . In this world of wooden shacks

and black ice, of pine forests and iron ore, the Alcazar was romance and color, beauty, warmth, gayety. To the lumberjacks and sooty miners of Iron Ridge the hard-faced girls, big hipped, broad of bosom, were houris in paradise. . . .

Once the curtain was up, they gazed at the naive show in silence. They viewed the girls in tights, mature women . . . in their late twenties or thirties. They gave themselves fancy names, usually with a French prefix—Minnie Le Claire, Belle Larue, Gracie LaMotte. . . . Such actresses that as were not for the moment on stage mingled with the audience, selling beer at a dollar a bottle. . . . They smiled woodenly and kept a sharp eye out for small change.

Another attraction the frontier held for women was the one forecast by Catharine Beecher: In the East, the ratio of men to women was nearly equal, but the frontier had a scarcity of women until well into the twentieth century. In 1865 there were four men to every woman in Washington Territory, and Nevada and Colorado were even more predominantly male. On their own or tempted by "excursions"—such as the one planned in 1866 by the president of Washington Territory's university, Asa S. Mercer, who collected about four hundred women willing to emigrate as teachers, housekeepers, and "husband hunters" and brought them west on a chartered steamship—young women followed the frontier to find romance and adventure. The railroads flooded the eastern states with pamphlets and ads pointing out "when a daughter of the East is once beyond the Missouri, she rarely recrosses it except on a bridal tour."

For whatever reason they had gone west, once there, women adopted means of coping with a difficult environment. The pioneers were both self-reliant and cooperative. They could "make do" in sod houses along the prairies, spending their snowbound winters without seeing anything beyond winter-locked houses, barns, and sheds, and at the same time they maintained a strong attitude of community. Communal silos were built by groups of farmers; harvesting meant that neighbors traveled from one farm to another to help gather crops.

Like the early colonists in the East, the pioneers first used the barter system: A farm woman might do laundry for bachelors and widowers in exchange for their help at harvesttime. But as time went on, jobs were paid for with money, and farm wives and daughters took part-time work such as running post offices from their kitchens, or setting up small butter-and-egg businesses to earn a few extra dollars.

"The girls I knew were always helping to pay for ploughs and reapers, brood-sows or steers to fatten," Willa Cather wrote in her novel *My Ántonia*, whose setting is Minnesota. Work on the farms was limited to the unpaid labor one did at home, or to assisting other farmers as "hired girls." In the industrial East and the South, domestic work was done mainly by immigrants or the free black women whose forebears were slaves; but paid household work in the West was the job of native-born farmers' daughters. As small towns sprang up along the frontier, there was other work, too. Soon there were milliners, dressmakers, clerks in country stores, and of course teachers in one-room schoolhouses.

The West was called "man's country," but in at least one place women held sway: the schoolhouse. The idea of free public education spread from the East across the plains, and when the new communities on the frontiers set up schoolhouses, the farmers chose women to teach their children. The value of a man's work as farmhand or artisan was high; young women could be hired for little more than "room and board."

The schoolmarms needed no formal education in the early days of westward expansion, for it was not until 1907 that Indiana became the first state to require all licensed teachers to be high-school graduates. Many of the women had, in fact, no more than basic grounding in reading, writing, arithmetic, American history, and geography. What they did need was plenty of spunk, for the one-room schoolhouse was a challenging experience.

Nearly always, the schoolteacher was required to be unmarried. She generally boarded with a family who lived near the school. Although she paid for her lodging, she had little independence. The families were expected to keep a watchful eye on the young woman's morals.

Teaching in a one-room schoolhouse meant running a half dozen or so classes simultaneously. The littlest children, seated in front close to the stove (which was lighted in the morning and kept stoked by the teacher, for there were no custodians in those simple buildings), might be learning the alphabet or chalking numbers on their slates, with a damp rag nearby to erase mistakes. Another group of children, a little more advanced, might be reading from a primer. There might be a geography lesson in progress, taught by the teacher from maps that rolled up when they were not in use, or perhaps a class in arithmetic, where the students learned "sums."

Although at least a basic education has always been considered a necessity in the American society, frontier children did not find attendance in school easy. In the spring and fall older children were kept home to help with planting and sowing. But in the winter a teacher might find herself in charge of a classroom filled with hulking farmhands older than she. There was nothing to do on long cold winter days, and sometimes "sitting in"—and "acting up"—on a pretty young schoolteacher's class was considered fun.

That the schoolteachers managed as well as they did is a triumph of spirit and resourcefulness. They taught older children to help with the younger ones—"each one teach one" was an early method of teacher help. But still, in spite of all the hardships of teaching in a bare wooden building where the space next to the stove was sweltering and the back of the room freezing, where water was drawn from an outdoor pump, toilet facilities were outhouses, and dark afternoons were illuminated by kerosene lamps that smoked and gave off noxious fumes—there was no shortage of young women eager to replace the teachers who left to marry, or to fill jobs newly created by an expanding population.

From the ranks of those plucky schoolmarms came the nucleus of a Western women's rights movement. Unlike women in the East, the pioneer suffragists worked without organizations to back them, often without even co-workers. Independent, accustomed to planning their own lives without the restrictions of propriety that the older, more established communities placed on women, the pioneer suffragists were free to draw convictions from their own life experiences, and to act directly to redress inequities they themselves encountered.

One such woman was Abigail Scott Duniway, who was to lead the fight for woman's suffrage in the Northwest. Abigail had come to Oregon on a wagon train in 1852. The trip from Illinois had been hazardous, and her mother, weakened by childbirth and already an invalid, died of cholera in the Black Hills of Dakota. The job of raising the children fell upon seventeen-year-old Abigail.

In spite of her home duties, Abigail was able to hold down a job teaching in a one-room Oregon schoolhouse. It was, for all its hard work, a happy time in her life. Her pay was meager, but it was hers to spend as she liked, and if she knew about the grievances of women in the East and their efforts to attain equal rights, it all bore little relationship to her own life.

Abigail's freedom and independence were not to last long. She married, went to live, as she wrote later, in a

> neighborhood composed chiefly of bachelors, who found comfort in mobilizing at meal times at the homes of the few married men in the township. . . . I, if not washing, scrubbing, or nursing the baby, was preparing their meals in our lean-to kitchen. To bear two children in two and a half years from my marriage day, to make thousands of pounds of butter every year for market not including what was used in our free hotel at home, to sew and cook, and wash and iron; to bake and clean and stew and fry; to be, in short, a general pioneer drudge, with never a penny of my own, was not pleasant business for an erstwhile school teacher.

Marriage brought other hard lessons to the feisty former schoolmarm. As a married woman she found that her destiny was inalterably linked with the success or failure of her partner. Her husband was in frail health, and a poor businessman to boot. The farm they worked together was lost—her share as well as his—because he signed three notes for a friend. While her signature was not required in granting the loan, under Oregon law she was equally responsible for the default. When the friend did not meet the loan, Abigail's farm was placed on the block and sold.

Support for the family, by then seven members, fell upon Abigail. Her husband was defeated, the family penniless. Abigail moved herself and her family to Portland. Determined to make full legal equality her life work, she begged and borrowed enough money to launch a progressive newspaper, which she called *The New Northwest*.

The New Northwest began as a modest enterprise, with its readers spread in straggling communities over a vast area. As writer, reformer, wage earner, Abigail Scott Duniway worked tirelessly. While much of her life is shadowy—like many other creative people she was inclined to embellish the facts in her personal life—there is nothing murky about her accounts of regional social history. Her vivid accounts of the embryonic women's rights movement remain an important source of information today. She traveled thousands of miles by stagecoach, riverboat, horse-drawn sleigh, to campaign for her cause. Women, she insisted, had to obtain the vote, contractual and legal rights such as the power to sign wills and deeds, to have full possession of their earnings, and in short to secure the rewards of their own labors.

Although Abigail Scott Duniway was the Northwest's most successful campaigner for woman suffrage—some sixty years after she first arrived in the Oregon Territory, she wrote the woman-suffrage proclamation for the State of Oregon—it was another working woman, Esther Morris, who linked suffrage with antidiscrimination laws and quietly pushed them through to passage by an all-male territorial legislature.

Esther Morris was a tall, strong-featured woman who knew how to earn her own living. She had conducted a successful millinery business in Oswego, New York, her birthplace. Widowed young, she moved to Illinois, where her first husband had left property to her. There she remarried, and when her husband and three sons decided to go to Wyoming, she once again packed her belongings and went west.

Esther Morris had more than a passing interest in women's rights by the time she arrived in Wyoming. While living in Illinois, she had attended a meeting where she heard Susan B. Anthony's cool, logical presentation of the need for suffrage and equal wages and opportunity. In the East, Mrs. Morris might have turned her talents toward organizing women in industry. In Wyoming, the only sizeable group of women who worked for wages was the schoolteachers, and Mrs. Morris' first order of business was an inquiry into pay scales for men and women in education. What she discovered was that even on the frontier, the same differences in wages prevailed in industry as in the developed sections of the country!

Taking advantage of the open friendliness of the new

territory, Mrs. Morris invited a group of community leaders and legislators to her home. She met—and gained the confidence of—a politician named William H. Bright, whose wife was a strong suffragist. Mrs. Morris persuaded her new friend to run for election for the presidency of the territorial council on a platform that included property rights for married women, equal pay for teachers of both sexes, and the vote for every citizen.

Bright won the election and kept his promise to the women who had backed him. His bills, although hotly contested, passed in the legislature in 1869. For the first time, American women had made their government responsible to them by guaranteeing both citizenship and equal pay for equal work.

The Wyoming elections of 1870 and 1871, the first in which American women participated fully, proved a disappointment to critics of women's rights, who hoped to find their prophecy of pandemonium fulfilled when women appeared at the polls. Instead, the elections went off in an orderly fashion, as reported by a New England minister who had recently arrived in Wyoming:

> I saw the rough mountaineers maintaining the most respectful decorum whenever the women approached the polls. . . . I was compelled to allow that in this new country, supposed at that time to be infested by hordes of cut-throats, gamblers and abandoned characters, I had witnessed a more quiet election than it had been my fortune to see in the quiet towns of Vermont [where only men could vote]. I saw ladies . . . ride to the place of voting, and alight in the midst of a silent crowd, and pass

through an open space to the polls, depositing their votes with no more exposure to insult or injury than they would expect on visiting a grocery store or meat market.

The furor, rather than being created by woman suffrage, was a result of a concomitant of the suffrage law: Once women were allowed to vote, their names were added to the lists of registered voters, and they automatically became eligible for jury duty. The thought of women in the jury box, exercising the "male" abilities to use logic and cool reason in making legal decisions, "so inflamed" some husbands, according to an account in *The History of Woman Suffrage*, which was edited by Elizabeth Cady Stanton, Susan B. Anthony and Matilda Joslyn Gage (Rochester, N.Y., 1881–86), "that they declared they would never live with their wives again if they served on the jury." There is no further word on whether the men carried through this threat, but when the issue came up before Chief Justice J. H. Howe of the Laramie City Court in 1870, he decided each woman had to determine for herself whether she wished to serve, and only one woman withdrew.

The battle for equality was to continue for the next generation, for when Wyoming appealed to Congress for statehood in 1890, congressional opponents of woman suffrage balked, claiming that admitting a full-suffrage state to the Union would extend the practice. Territorial delegate Joseph M. Carey wired home to the legislature the news that Wyoming might have to compromise by abandoning its suffrage rights. "We will remain out of the Union a hundred years rather than come in without the women!" the territorial legislature wired back. When on July 23, 1890, Wyoming celebrated its new statehood in Cheyenne, the flag honoring the occasion was given by the Governor to Esther Morris, "the mother of woman suffrage in Wyoming."

Despite the furor over the vote in Wyoming, once female suffrage was introduced in the West, there was no turning the tide. In Colorado, then Utah, women won the vote. Carrie Chapman Catt, a new figure in the movement, campaigned across the West and was instrumental in bringing woman suffrage to Idaho in 1896. At the end of the century, some twenty years before the passage of the Nineteenth Amendment in which all American women won the vote, there were four states where women went to the polls on Election Day.

In other ways, women in the West continued to move toward equality. Although the first married women's property act was passed in New York State as early as 1836, wives' rights in the East varied from state to state and, at best, were far short of those attained by Western women. By 1900, in every single Western state, wives could own and control their separate property, could dispose of such property in their wills; and if a wife engaged in business by herself or went outside the home to work, her earnings were her own. In eight states—all in the West except for Louisiana—property acquired by husband and wife during their marriage belonged equally to both.

Equal pay for equal work fared less well. Despite its promising beginnings in Wyoming, the concept did not spread to other states, nor for that matter even to professions or employment other than schoolteaching. It wasn't until 1961 that both Wisconsin and Hawaii enacted legislation guaranteeing men and women the same pay scales.

As the century ended, women in the West could look back to solid achievement in their efforts for equality. More than that, they pioneered a concept that was to become increasingly important during the twentieth century: They had brought their grievances to the seat of government, and through the law itself had secured citizenship and property guarantees. They set the stage for the next battle—now, once again, to take place in the urban centers of the East. It would not be long in coming.

7

An Era of Reform

Mark Twain called the end of the nineteenth century "The Gilded Age."

At one end of the scale were the fabled "400"—in actuality some four thousand millionaires—who controlled the pyramiding wealth of the nation; at the other, what a soon-to-be-reformer named Josephine Lowell called the "five hundred thousand," those wage earners in New York in 1889, "two hundred thousand of them women and children, and seventy-five thousand of those working under dreadful conditions or for starvation wages."

A battle was in the making—a conflict between huge profits and human rights. At the core were women—women who were the victims of America's booming new industrialism, but also women who were catalysts of an age of reform that profoundly changed our society, leaving a legacy of social-protest movement, agencies of social welfare such as visiting nurses, and settlement houses, powerful labor unions, protective legislation restricting the abuse of labor by employers, a body of antitrust laws, and finally the concept that it was the state itself that was responsible for safeguarding the citizens with respect to working conditions, hours, health, wages, and danger to life itself.

The background to the reform movement was a period of the most rapid financial growth in American history. The years after Reconstruction brought the North unparalleled prosperity. From Washington, D.C., to the North, and all across the plains states, the nation's businesses boomed. Oil gushed from the wells of Pennsylvania and Ohio. A web of railway lines was built to span the continent, linking the cities of the North, carrying cattle to the slaughterhouses of Chicago and St. Louis, grain from the West to Eastern mills to be ground, shipped, and distributed. The textile mills in New England ran twenty-four-hour shifts; clothing manufacture took over whole sections of New York City.

America became a nation of cities, commerce, and industry. New York's population had grown from one million to one and a half million between 1880 and 1890. Philadelphia and Chicago passed the million mark. Electric trolley cars hummed along miles of newly laid tracks. Overhead, telephone and electric wires crisscrossed. Horseless carriages—electrics and steamers and now and again a gasoline-powered automobile—sped along city streets at the unheard-of speed of fifteen miles an hour, crowding out horse-drawn vehicles.

Inside the office buildings—some of them tall "skyscrapers" of as many as twenty stories—a new technology served the needs of commerce and industry. The old systems of handwritten accounts could not handle the rising volume of office work. In the early eighteenth century an Englishman named Henry Mill had patented an idea for "an artificial machine for the impressing of letters." A century later the idea was taken up by three men from Milwaukee, and in 1873 a contract was made with E. Remington & Sons, Gunmakers, for the first typewriter to be placed on the market in 1874. At the same time, Alexander Graham Bell's innovative "talking machine" became the telephone. In 1878 the first telephone switchboard, in New Haven, Connecticut, went into operation. In 1888 there were sixty thousand typewriters in use, along with efficient new office machines of other types.

Lining the fashionable "avenues" in the cities were large retail establishments—the new "department stores." Gone were the old general stores, with their stocks of housewares, yard goods, and notions all sold behind one counter by an aproned storekeeper who was salesclerk, wrapper, and cashier all at once. At Lord & Taylor and Macy's in New York, Marshall Field in Chicago, Strawbridge & Clothier in Philadelphia, merchandise was separated into divisions and departments. These were supervised by individual divisional managers and department buyers. Advertising, service, buying, and accounting were each separate operations.

Most of all, there were changes in the crowds that hurried to work every morning along the bustling city streets. No longer were the business districts all-male preserves. Now there were women, thousands of them, in their plain serge skirts, neat shirtwaists, and high-buttoned shoes—saleswomen, cashiers, wrappers, typists, bookkeepers, stenographers—the advance guard of the coming hordes of female white-collar workers.

As each new field opened, creating a need for a large labor pool, more and more women moved into the working world. The figures tell the story: In 1900, while there were still some 700,000 women who were categorized as "farm laborers and managers," among the more than five million wage-earning women the vast majority were employed *off* the farm.

The largest group of women—some 1,800,000—worked in domestic occupations for families other than their own. There were laundresses, cooks, maids, and other household workers. Schoolteaching absorbed another large segment of the female working population: There were 325,000 teachers. Factory work continued as a major source of employment: There were some 671,000 in clothing and garment trades, and 261,000 in textile manufacturing. In addition, there were some 200,000 office workers, and more than 100,000 retail salesclerks.

But far more significant than the vastly increased numbers of women who now were part of the workforce was the fact that for the first time in American history, a large group of workers from the middle classes joined the poor farmers' daughters, immigrants, and members of minority groups working outside their homes. A generation earlier, middle-class girls could teach school or "help mother" until potential husbands appeared to woo and win them. Now, large-scale industry and commerce opened a variety of jobs to young women, and by the hundreds of thousands they joined brothers and fathers in the working force.

The entrance of women in force, particularly unmarried women (for only among the black and immigrant populations was a large majority of wives employed outside the home), brought with it attendant problems. The morality of the time insisted that a woman's "special calling" was to be a wife and mother. There was the fear that in going into the outside world, women would lose their "womanliness," their wish to fulfill the wife-mother role that was "God's purpose in creating women." In the case of young girls there was another fear. Removed from the watchful eye of a parent, a girl might be "led astray"—down the path of sexual immorality. The "sweet innocence" of unmarried girls was in jeopardy. Indeed, a popular song of the time implored that "Heaven Help the Working Girl" to resist temptation!

The society at large was unprepared for the entrance of large numbers of women into the working force. If women were to become wage earners, dependent upon themselves for their own livings, they would need safe, inexpensive housing. If they were to become part of the new technology, they needed technical training—typing, shorthand, bookkeeping. If they were to work in factories and industries in which their health might be jeopardized, they needed governmental protection. If women were, indeed, the "mothers of the race," something had to be done to insure that they would not ruin their health so that they could not fulfill this "natural function." Beyond that, working women required a wide range of social services—medical care, child care, and other aid and protection that no agency, charity, or governmental facility had yet offered.

The society was in conflict. On one hand, American

industry required vast numbers of workers, and women were the obvious pool from which labor could be drawn. On the other hand, old prejudices provided the means by which women could be discriminated against. Clearly, if something was to be done to help, it would have to be done by women themselves!

The first women to step into the void were two British gentlewomen who, unknown to each other, organized separately in 1855. Emma Robarts started a prayer union, dedicated to the spiritual uplift of "princesses . . . domestic servants, and factory girls," while Lady Kinnaird opened homes and institutes for nurses returning from the Crimean War. The two groups eventually merged, to become the Young Women's Christian Association. That same year, in New York, thirty-five women met to form a Ladies' Christian Association, with a view toward providing for the "temporal, moral and religious welfare of young women who are dependent on their own exertions for support." The idea was taken up by another group of women, this time Bostonians, in 1866. They wrote a constitution and formally organized as the Young Women's Christian Association.

The YWCA was the first organization to recognize the profound effects of the Industrial Revolution on the lives of women, and to attempt to provide services that neither the educational system, government, nor business itself was prepared to offer. At the turn of the century there were hundreds of YWCA chapters, many of them in buildings that offered low-cost housing for working women. The association sponsored classes in commercial education so that working women could upgrade skills, courses in health and hygiene, and recreational programs—dances, athletic contests, summer camps, cultural events. As an organization that provided self-help and social, intellectual, and moral guidance to working women, the YWCA was, from its very beginning, an important force. It did not, however, direct itself to issues such as working conditions, wages, hours. To improve the lot of working women in these areas, other organizations would have to be formed.

There were a number of embryo groups already in existence from which a nucleus could be drawn to make up a movement devoted to the cause of the working woman. First, there were women's clubs—church groups, literary societies, charitable organizations. Women had organized as abolitionists, and in temperance societies—organizations that worked to make the use of alcohol illegal. There was a growing suffrage movement, already beginning to taste victory in the West and looking toward further gains in the rest of the country. There were women's trade unions; and while it was true that they were handicapped by lack of funds and sustaining membership, they had the potential power to be a force around which working women could rally. And finally there was the settlement movement—Hull House in Chicago, the Henry Street Settlement in New York, founded on the order of Toynbee Hall in London to "provide education and the means of recreation and enjoyment for the people in the poorer districts of . . . great cities; to enquire into the condition of the poor and to . . . advance plans . . . to promote their welfare." What was to emerge from these groups was a coalition—heiresses and wives of industrialists with the means to devote their lives to a cause; educated women with the knowledge and background to lend vision to the cause; and working women themselves, with the life experience to keep the movement down to earth.

As early as 1886, a group of New York women decided:

> For united effort there is a need of a Central Society which shall gather together those already devoted to the cause of organization among women, shall collect statistics and publish facts, shall be ready to furnish information and advice, and above all, shall continue and increase agitation on this subject.

A likely place to start, the women decided, was in the burgeoning new retail industry, where thousands of women were shunted into the lowest-paid, most menial positions: wrappers, waitresses in the stores' tea rooms and employees' cafeterias, salesclerks in the "budget departments," while men moved rapidly into supervisory and managerial positions. In 1895 E. W. Bloomingdale, the president of the New York department store that bore his name, declared proudly that his establishment did not employ a single woman who performed the same tasks as a man. The organization promptly appointed Alice Woodbridge, a former retail salesclerk, to conduct a survey of working conditions in New York stores and find out what was going on.

Alice Woodbridge outlined a course of action. Under her direction a squad of women volunteers went into department stores, asked sales help about wages, hours, benefits. Working undercover, they unearthed a pattern of discrimination and exploitation so clear that their findings sparked the influential women to whom they brought the report into immediate action.

The group of well-to-do women who pored over Alice Woodbridge's report were organized under the banner of the Consumers League. They included reformers such as Josephine Lowell, who had turned from pauper relief and prison reform because she believed "if the working people had all they ought to have, we should not have paupers and criminals. It is better to save them before they go under, than to spend your life fishing them out when they're half-drowned and taking care of them afterwards."

Maud Nathan, too, was a rich woman with a social conscience. Although she lived in a fashionable New York brownstone house where she had four servants, she prided herself on her "womanly skills." She supervised the dressmaking in her house, and once a year retreated to the basement kitchen for two weeks' labor over hot kettles, putting up a year's supply of preserves, pickles, corned beef. Lest she be criticized for abandoning her housewife's duties in favor of community work, all during her presidency of the Consumers League, Mrs. Nathan took pains to make her home "the finest house in New York."

From their vantage point as privileged women Mrs. Lowell, Mrs. Nathan, and the other members of their committee saw the buying public as being able to exert the most pressure and finally being able to create most change in the conditions confronting working women. This was their reasoning: Working women themselves had very little power, for, as the League reported in 1895: "They are all women; and consequently usually timid and unaccustomed to associated action." Further-more, the retail clerks were "young, many being between the ages of fourteen and twenty; and therefore without the wisdom, strength of character, or experience which would enable them to act in their own behalf." Finally, "their trade, although it has highly skilled departments, is mostly unskilled, and therefore there is an almost un-limited supply of applicants for their situations in case they do not accept the conditions offered them."

The buying public—the consumers—held the power, the League thought. If women shoppers would boycott the stores that underpaid and overworked their clerks, management would be forced to meet standards estab-lished by the League. The League set to work to prepare a "White List"—a roster of stores that complied with the League's "Standards of Fair House." To get on the approved list, a store had to pay a weekly minimum of six dollars to each of its employees; restrict work to a ten-hour day with forty-five minutes for lunch; provide a week's paid vacation; make available comforts such as lunchrooms, seats behind the counters, and lockers to store the employees' coats and hats; and above all, not employ anybody under the age of fourteen.

The publication of the first "White List" was a rousing success. Only eight stores in New York passed the stringent requirements. The buying public flocked to support these establishments, at the same time refusing to deal with shops that did not comply with the League's requirements. Seeing their profits shrink and their com-petitors enriched, New York department stores quickly moved to correct workers' complaints.

The New York Consumers League was encouraged by

its success. Under the direction of Mrs. Lowell, and later Mrs. Nathan, the League grew until there were affiliates in twenty states. From agitation for reform in retail stores, the organization went on to insist on similar standards in employing women engaged in clothing manufacture and in processing some food products, such as milk. Eventually the League—now the National Consumers League—moved on to pressing for governmental responsibility in limiting the number of hours that women could be made to work, and in other areas concerning health and safety standards.

While the Consumers League concentrated on using moral pressure to secure working women's rights, another agency of social change, the settlement movement, played a different role in the lives of working women. The educated, idealistic men and women who went directly into the slums to work with the poor found out firsthand what life was for people whose wages could not cover their basic needs. Here Jane Addams, a sheltered young woman who after her graduation from Rockford Seminary, in Illinois, traded her comfortable, middle-class life to found a settlement house in Chicago's slums, describes the community Hull House served:

"The streets are inexpressibly dirty, the number of schools inadequate . . . many houses have no water supply save the faucet in the backyard, and there are no fire escapes." Each flat in the tenements was crowded with several families. Many also served as "sweatshops," where women and children and sometimes men, too, did piecework on clothing for pennies a unit.

Hull House set out to fill all the gaps in the deprived lives of the poor and working classes. Jane Addams and her associates set up adult-education classes to teach immigrants to speak and read and write English. They gave lectures and demonstrations on hygiene, child care, home nursing, preventive medicine, and nutrition. Anticipating the need for child-care centers to provide safe shelter for the children of working mothers, they ran nursery schools and after-school programs. Facing the fact that many young women chose prostitution as an alternative to working in sweatshops and factories for wages so low that they would not be able to pay for food, shelter, and clothing, Hull House concentrated on vocational training and guidance.

Training women for better jobs brought home to the settlement-house leaders the problems of working women. It brought them into contact with working women who were actively trying to organize labor. Lillian Wald, a visiting nurse on New York's poverty-stricken Lower East Side who was later to found the Henry Street Settlement, describes her own introduction to trade unionism when a young woman who lived in the same apartment house came to visit:

> Our visit was mingled with consternation to learn that she wished aid in organizing a trades union. Even the term was unknown to me. She spoke without bitterness of the troubles of her shop-mates, and tried to make me see why they thought a union would bring them relief. It was evident that she came to me because one who spoke English so easily would know how to organize in the 'American Way.' . . . The next day I managed to find

time to visit the library for academic information on the subject of trades unions.

Mary McDowell, the director of Chicago's University Settlement, did not have to go to a library to find out what a trade union was. The University Settlement was located in the "back of the yards"—the area in Chicago in which cattle is slaughtered and packed—and Miss Mc-Dowell worked directly with the union in its organiza-tion of men. It did not take long for her to realize that women, too, needed to belong to unions. In 1903 she made a speech to Chicago Club men criticizing union leadership for failing to reach out to women employees.

Mary McDowell did not save her criticism for men. She told women that they must follow the lead of male blue-collar workers in organizing. She went further: She sent for Michael Donnelly, the leader of the stockyard unions, and asked for help, and then she and two young women who worked in the yards organized Local No. 183 of the Amalgamated Meat Cutters and Butchers Workmen of North America. The local unit lasted only a year (it disappeared when an unsuccessful strike in 1904 wiped out all the stockyard unions for a time), but it was successful in uniting working women of diverse na-tionalities—German, Irish, Polish, black—and the edu-cated, professional leadership in the settlement-house movement.

Mary McDowell's successful foray directly into the world of working women prepared the stage for the next development—the final coming together of a sister-hood composed of representatives of women from every walk of life, organized on the basis of common femininity, around one common cause: the improvement of life for working women. There were unionists, feminists, wealthy women disenchanted with conventional philanthropies and social reform activities, women in the settlement movement, native-born women, immigrants, representatives of Working Girls' Clubs and YWCAs. Unlike earlier coalitions, the Women's Trade Union League, or WTUL, as the organization was called, concentrated on dollars-and-cents issues through the means of trade-union organization.

Gertrude Barnum, a leading upper-class member in the League's early years, describes her own evolution, which paralleled that of the new movement:

> I myself have graduated from the Settlement into the trade union. . . . I began to feel that . . . the work was not fundamental. It introduced into working women's lives books and flowers and music . . . it gave them a place to meet and see their friends or leave their babies when they went out to work, but it did not raise their wages or shorten their hours. It began to dawn on me, therefore, that it would be more practical to turn our energies toward raising wages and shortening hours.

Leonora O'Reilly, another founder, came into the Women's Trade Union League by a different route. Her parents came to America with the waves of Irish immigrants during the famine. Her father, a printer, died when his daughter was only a year old, and to support herself and the baby, Leonora's mother did piecework, bringing bundles of shirts from the factory to be finished at home. Leonora's wages were needed; when she was eleven she went to work in a New York collar factory, earning one dollar for a dozen collars. In three years the rate had declined to fifty cents a dozen, and Leonora joined the Knights of Labor to take part in a strike.

The strike of 1886 was the first of many that Leonora O'Reilly would participate in or organize. A fiery unionist, she came to the attention of influential women like Josephine Lowell of the Consumers League, who recognized her leadership qualities, paid off her debts, and gave her money so that she could go back to school. Education freed her from the long hours and drudgery of factory work. She was able to become a teacher at the Manhattan Trade School for Girls and eventually a full-time organizer for the Women's Trade Union League.

Leonora O'Reilly's job with the WTUL meant that she had to bring other, smaller unions into the coalition. Some were independent unions—small groups of women who worked in industries such as millinery, cleaning and dyeing, and cigarette or paper-goods manufacture. These tended to be poorly organized and functioned only sporadically. Another kind were called "federal locals." These were limited to women in one trade, and were organized under the banner of the American Federation of Labor. But although the federal unions carried a prestigious affiliation, they actually fared badly. Unlike the men's locals, which were composed of highly skilled workers such as plumbers and carpenters, the women's groups were made up of low-paid, unskilled trades-women. The union itself felt that the women's groups did not share the general interests of the greater federation, and gave scant attention to women's efforts to become active unionists.

Outspoken Leonora O'Reilly, who thought of herself first as a feminist and secondly a trade unionist, decided that the traditionalist attitudes of labor leaders such as Samuel Gompers, head of the American Federation of Labor, were no loss to women. "I want to say this to my sisters," she told a WTUL convention. "For mercy's sakes, let us be *glad* if men don't help us." It was *women* she wanted to see taking charge of their own lives, and she went directly to the immigrant women who were organizing in the needle trades—the industries involved in manufacture of clothing—to bring grass-roots leaders such as Rose Schneiderman and Pauline Newman of the newly formed International Ladies' Garment Workers' Union into the WTUL fold.

The first test of the WTUL's strength came in 1909, in response to the grievances of women in the shirtwaist-making industry in New York. The shirtwaist makers' work was insecure, seasonal, subject to layoffs, with no job security or benefits; wages were pitifully low; working conditions in the factories were nearly intolerable. On a day-to-day basis the women were harassed—fined for small infractions, not permitted time for lunch or rest periods, granted no overtime for work that sometimes stretched a working day to fourteen hours. At last, after a series of strikes and other job actions that had come to little, a mass meeting of the shirtwaist workers was called on November 22. The decision to hold a "general strike," with participation by all the union's members, was made that night.

The strike's planners had hoped that three thousand workers would support it. Instead, ten thousand women covered their machines and went home to wait it out. The strike, called the "Revolt of the Thirty Thousand," required picket lines, strike relief, welfare aid. Twenty-four halls had to be hired for the strikers' meetings, with speakers at each in Yiddish, Italian, and English. The WTUL went into the strike as a loosely knit confederation of concerned women. It emerged, tempered by the fire of the crisis, an efficient organization, truly competent to represent a broad coalition of working women.

When the excitement of the strike died down, the WTUL appraised its position. The mass support for the action had proved that women could be organized in trade unions, could be counted on to work toward a greater gain at the cost of temporary sacrifice, could enlist the support of the public at large toward the cause. Never again would the cry be raised: "Women can't be organized"!

More important to the cause of working women was the fact that the strike pointed out directions for the future. Only two out of one hundred women were unionized, and even under optimum conditions it would be years before a sizeable majority of working women could be organized within trades. In the meantime, "the sisterhood"—the coalition of women who came together in the WTUL—had accumulated experience and know-how in stirring up public opinion, in dealing with business, labor, and the government itself. Why not use this experience to gain immediate and widespread guarantees for the issues women were fighting for through unions—a minimum wage, maximum hours, job safety—through the government itself? In order that *all* women workers be protected, not just those who were unionized, the decision was made to direct all efforts toward protective laws.

A group of pioneer social workers trained in the settlement movement, primarily under the guidance of Jane Addams, used their direct access to women workers to investigate factories and offices, questioning clerks, machine operators, saleswomen, about job conditions. A committee of women, including Mary McDowell, lobbied in Congress for a national investigation. Backed by sympathetic President Theodore Roosevelt, the committee obtained a congressional grant. The result—a nineteen-volume report that took four years to complete—became the basis for decades of legislation concerning women and children as workers.

By 1907, some twenty states had legislation limiting, in some industries, the working hours of women. The laws were tested when the Supreme Court agreed to hear a case concerning the hours of women laundry workers: Curt Muller vs. The State of Oregon. Using data gathered earlier by the congressional investigators, the court considered evidence that showed the injurious effects of long hours on young women, of overwork during pregnancy and after, for mothers, children, and future generations. It was a landmark case, for it was decided on medical, psychological, and sociological evidence instead of legal precedent.

The number of laws safeguarding working women grew rapidly over the years. Eventually there were laws in some thirty-six states limiting the maximum number of hours women could work. While these laws served an important initial purpose, they finally became obsolete. Fair-labor laws that apply to all workers—both men and women—were enacted. Neither men nor women are now required to work twelve or fourteen hours a day, for example, and the need for safety measures in jobs involving physical danger has come to be seen as equally important for workers of both sexes.

Ironically, the very laws that were deemed so important for women's welfare early in the century have been found to be discriminatory in recent years, and the trend has been to have them removed from the books. For example, women have been kept out of jobs on the grounds that they could not lift heavy weights; work at night and overtime work, with their higher pay, have been restricted. However, there is no denying that the legislation, as well as other gains made by women during the age of reform, served an important purpose.

On balance, the coalition of women who agitated for social reform did more than eliminate the terrible conditions of the sweatshops and the glaring inequalities between men's and women's labor that they set out to correct. They ended forever a disregard for the humanity of working people—the placid acceptance of the working woman as either a machine or a beast of burden. They introduced a concept of the working person as a full human being possessed of needs and frailties, basic rights and legitimate ambitions, into what had until then been the cruel impersonality of the industrial marketplace.

8

Women in the Professions

The pioneer professionals were valiant women. Old records give clues about the hardships endured by women such as Mrs. Whitmore, whose work was delivering the babies of settlers around Marlboro, Vermont. "Mrs. Whitmore was very useful . . . both as nurse and as a midwife," her obituary, in 1763, reads. "She possessed a vigorous constitution, and frequently travelled through the woods on snowshoes, from one part of the town to another, both by night and day, to relieve the distressed. She lived to age 87, officiated at more than 2,000 births, and never lost a patient."

In the early days of American history, medicine, nursing, the care of the sick either by men or women, was largely a matter of circumstance. Midwives delivered babies and cared for new mothers, sometimes taking their fees in goods and other times simply performing neighborly service. Samuel Fuller, the doctor of Plymouth, had been a silk maker in England, and John Winthrop the younger, Governor of Connecticut, gave medical advice to his friends in person, diagnosed distant patients' illnesses by letter, and bought remedies for them when he was in London on diplomatic business. Herbs and folk medicine were brewed by men and women over their own hearth fires. There were neither medical schools nor pharmaceutical courses, and the simple remedies of the day—"powders," "tar-water," salves, and unctions—were as likely to be prescribed and compounded by women as by men.

Neither did law begin as a profession. The colonists were antilaw, in general. They brought with them the tradition of English common law, but they had little love or respect for it. They had suffered too much under its limitation of their religious freedom—and, indeed, had fled to the New World to escape it. The colonies simply drew up their own codes and scriptures, used no lawbooks, allowed laymen to administer a kind of natural fairness. Although in the eighteenth century something like a professional bar gradually developed, with many of its leaders studying under a system called Inns of Court, it was not until 1779—three years after the Revolution—that William and Mary College established the first professorship of law in the New World.

There was, however, one profession that even in the early days of our country met the definition as we now know it. It was, of course, the ministry. And from this "learned profession," women in America were carefully excluded.

The first test of woman's place in the religious life of the colonies challenged not only woman's role but the Puritan beliefs about religious salvation, about the authority of church and state, and finally resulted in the formation of a new settlement. It all revolved around the stalwart figure of Anne Hutchinson.

Anne Hutchinson was born in England in 1593, the daughter of a clergyman. She and her husband, William, emigrated to Boston to seek religious freedom. But in the New World, as in the old, she found religion hemmed in by authority. Anne had come to believe that each person could communicate directly with God without the intervention of the church and ministry, for she thought that God existed in every human being. This faith, the "Covenant of Grace," demanded equality for herself and everybody else. Just as this theology had challenged the Stuart kings and sent "heretics" such as herself to America, it now challenged the powers of the Massachusetts Bay Colony. When Anne, well known and loved for her skills as a nurse and nature healer, began to gather devoted disciples around her for weekly prayer meetings, she headed straight into conflict with the local ministers—and more important, since there was no separation of church and state, with the governors of the colony.

The vengeance of the colony was swift and stern. Anne's unprecedented demand, that she—a woman—be allowed to think for herself about God, brought attack on two levels: through the civil court and by religious proceedings.

"A woman of haughty and fierce carriage," as her enemy, the elder Governor John Winthrop, described her, "of a nimble wit and active spirit, and a very voluble tongue, more bold than a man," she was scarcely at her best when she took the stand to defend herself, for she was pregnant and seriously ill. Unmoved by gallantry, the prosecution harassed her. She was denied the right to introduce evidence to support her position. Her witnesses were browbeaten and the judges declared in advance that they had already decided the case! The verdict came in—guilty as charged, with exile as punishment. Anne's question, "I desire to know wherefore I am banished," was met with this terse rejoinder from Governor Winthrop: "Say no more, the Court knows wherefore, and is satisfied."

Neither the civil trial nor the one that followed, a trial on the grounds of heresy which resulted in her excommunication from the church, broke Anne's spirit. Her power was still so strong that when she left the Boston colony for the wilderness of Roger Williams' Rhode Island settlement, thirty-five families followed her. Although she was not to live long (in her last search to establish a colony she migrated to what is now the outskirts of New York City, where she was killed in an Indian massacre), her influence endured. Her name today is synonymous with religious freedom.

Other women in Colonial religious life chose separate paths. The beginnings of the Methodist Church in America are traced to Philip Embury, an Irish immigrant, but actually his work was done in partnership with his cousin, Mrs. Barbara Heck. Methodist ministers, including John Wesley, had made missionary tours to the New World in order to establish Methodism in the colonies. But there was no church in New York until 1766, when Embury and Mrs. Heck, encouraged by their informal congregation of four people, decided to pick a site in lower Manhattan and construct their own.

Barbara Heck designed the church for "economy and

utility." The "economy" was assured by having Embury do much of the carpentry, while she herself white-washed the walls. The completed church attracted a growing congregation, and when in 1769 missionaries from England took charge, the Hecks moved to Salem, New York, where they established another church. Barbara Heck remained in the background, but after the Revolutionary War she, like a sizeable number of other colonists, emigrated to Canada. There she was again active in establishing Methodism in still another country on the new continent.

Anne Hutchinson headed directly into controversy, claiming her right to her own ministry. Barbara Heck preferred to work behind the scenes. A third path was taken by Mother Ann Lee, who set up her church as a separate community, outside the powers of both state and church.

The unlettered daughter of an English blacksmith, Ann Lee became a fervent believer in a small religious sect known as the French Prophets, derisively called "Shakers." Her many divine revelations convinced both herself and other Shakers that she was a prophet of God. One of her interpretations led the entire group to the colonies to establish the sect there. Mother Lee's teachings were based on the idea that God has a dual nature: The masculine aspect had already become manifest in Jesus, she taught. The second incarnation of the Holy Spirit would be a female. This millennial prophecy, she concluded, had at last been fulfilled—in the person of Ann Lee.

Mother Lee and eight disciples emigrated to New York in 1774. The utopian colony she set up soon attracted other converts, and was immediately self-supporting. Everyone worked hard at tasks assigned according to talent, not gender: raising herbs and developing seed strains that were sold outside the community, designing and building their own furniture and farm implements. No individual credit was given, but it is likely that women as well as men were responsible for such inventions as the wooden clothespin whose design was never improved, and for the beautiful furniture whose simple lines still serve as models for present-day designers.

Although the sect gave equal authority to women—after Mother Lee's death in 1784 the Shakers came under the joint leadership of Elder Joseph Meacham and Eldress Lucy Wright—it was able to overcome the initial opposition from society mainly because the practical aspect of the church was in keeping with the values of a Puritan society: hard work, thrift, and "Yankee ingenuity."

The American Revolution brought with it the separation of state and church. The position of women in religion became purely a matter to be decided within the individual church itself. Resting on a combination of tradition, stemming from what some theologians consider an antifeminist era in history that took place about fifty years after the death of Jesus, with a literal interpretation of the Bible, particularly the letters of St. Paul, ordination in the major religious bodies was entirely a male preserve. Women might serve as deaconesses or in other positions on a lay level. In the Catholic Church, women served as nuns, rising to high positions within their orders—the vast majority of female college presidents even today are nuns who administer Catholic colleges and universities—but not as priests. Women in America founded small sects and even one major movement, Christian Science, which was formally organized by Mary Baker Eddy in Boston in 1879. But it was not until more than two hundred years after Anne Hutchinson raised the issue that the question of whether organized religion could include women would once again arise.

In 1945, Episcopal Bishop James A. Pike of California recommended that Phyllis A. Edwards be ordained as a deacon. Although he was unsuccessful—it was not until 1970 that the Episcopal Church allowed women to sit as delegates in the highest policy-making body and gave deaconesses a wide range of church functions—the controversy stirred by Bishop Pike's gesture was once again in the public consciousness.

Other developments, too, began to cause the Protestant churches to redefine some of the functions of the ministry. Under the inspiration of the ecumenical movement begun by the Catholic Church after the Second World War, churches began to draw nearer to each other, to cut through the barriers that had separated various denominations. In America, many churches endorsed the civil rights movement and antipoverty measures. From within the churches themselves, as well as from outside, there came these questions: Was not the women's liberation movement built around the same general principles—democracy, antiexploitation, respect for individual rights? More than that, if the churches continued to discriminate against women, would they not lose their "relevance" to today's social problems?

Gradually, the numbers of women entering seminaries

and turning toward the pastoral ministry began to increase. In 1975 there were an estimated five thousand ordained women in the country. Among the top ten Christian churches in the United States, the United Methodist Church has admitted the largest number of ordained women—about five hundred. Not far behind is the United Presbyterian Church. Both branches of the Lutheran Church now ordain women, as does the Southern Baptist Convention. Two relatively small denominations, the United Church of Christ and the American Baptist Convention, have high proportions of woman clergy. There has been progress among the Jewish congregations, too. In recent years the Reconstructionist Rabbinical College in Philadelphia and the Hebrew Union College in Cincinnati opened their doors to women, and while there still is objection to women serving in full capacity, particularly in the Orthodox congregations, there are now female rabbis and cantors.

But while virtually all of the major denominations made commitments to women's equality in the past few years, and women, in turn, increased their percentage in major Protestant seminaries from about three to thirty-five between 1966 and 1976—more than one in three ministers-to-be is now a woman—the Episcopal Church, in which the modern battle was launched, hung in the balance. In 1973, at the General Convention, the House of Bishops approved a change that would allow the ordination of women, while the House of Deputies turned down the proposal. Since passage of a measure requires a majority in both houses, the proposal failed. Rebels within the church objected. In 1974 eleven women were "irregularly ordained" in Washington, D.C., and one of them, Betty Scheiss, who was denied a congregation on the basis of her sex, filed suit in Federal court, citing equal-employment legislation and seeking back pay and damages. At last the strident argument came up, for the final time, at the House of Deputies in September 1976.

The convention was packed, as priests, laymen, and laywomen came together in Minneapolis to determine once and for all whether women were to receive official ordination. One after another, more than fifty delegates rose to argue for and against the proposal. Against the opponents' contention that if Jesus had wanted women priests he would have named women as apostles, those in favor argued that Jesus chose only men because of the culture in which he lived, that times had changed and with them the cultural proscriptions against women. At last the vote was taken, and an eerie silence settled as the count was tallied. Then the decision: Episcopal women in America would be allowed into the priest-hood!

The last major holdout is the Catholic Church, which stands behind a position explained in *L'Osservatore Romano*, the official Vatican newspaper: "Christ did not . . . let women share the message He received from His Father. This is a fact and all we can do is recognize it." Nevertheless, signs of change are beginning to appear in ecumenical conferences, and the eighteen-hundred-member National Coalition of American Nuns endorsed the position that there is "no theological, sociological or biological reason for denying ordination to women."

While the struggle to open religious professions to women has been sporadic, there has been a steady onslaught against the barriers to women's entry in two other professions: medicine and law. Beginning with the successful battle waged by one exceptional woman who was willing to commit her life to what she saw as "a great moral struggle . . . a moral fight," the cause of women's equality in medicine has been continuous for more than a century.

Elizabeth Blackwell was well equipped to clear the path for other women. She was born into a family that heartily supported women's rights (one brother married suffragist Lucy Stone; another, Antoinette Brown). Her father died while she was young, leaving a family of eight, and Elizabeth was forced to support herself by teaching school, an occupation she disliked. "I wish I could devise some good way of maintaining myself," she wrote in her diary in 1837, when she was sixteen, "but all the restrictions which confine my dear sex render my aspirations useless." Finally she decided that, useless or not, she had to pursue her dream of being a doctor.

Elizabeth had plenty of time to review her decision. For two years she corresponded with leading doctors, pleading for help. She applied to twenty-nine medical schools, without a single acceptance. Always the reasons for her rejection were the same. Modesty, she was told, prohibited it; women were "too fine" to view the human body. They were "too frail" for the around-the-clock hours doctors had to keep. And of course, their intellects could not absorb any study as complicated as anatomy!

At last a small medical college in Geneva, New York, received Elizabeth's application. Trying to find a way out, the administrators put the decision up to the all-male student body, with the provision that a single blackball would keep her out. The students thought it would be a prank to admit a "female." To a man, they voted "yes," and sat back mischievously to await the girl who would be a joke on the administration.

Elizabeth's letters from that time make one wonder how she bore it! The other students alternately sniggered and made advances, landladies refused to rent the "freak" a room, townspeople pointed her out on the streets, and the professors were coolly condescending or sharply sarcastic. Elizabeth controlled her rage and hurt, and stuck it out to graduate at the head of her class on January 23, 1849.

Elizabeth Blackwell had hoped to become a surgeon. She applied to, and was accepted by, La Maternité, France's famous obstetric school; but an eye infection, which ultimately cost her the sight of one eye, ended that ambition. She went to England, to study with Florence Nightingale, instead. Her aim was to bring back to American patients the advanced ideas about sanitation and hygiene that the British nurse had developed.

Her first years back in New York found her no closer to success. No private patient would risk being treated by a "monster"; hospitals would not allow her into their wards or even dispensaries. "I understand now why this life has never been lived by another," she wrote. "It *is* hard . . . to live against every species of social opposition."

With no way to make a living as a physician, Dr. Blackwell gave a course of lectures on bodily hygiene and physical education for girls. Then her luck turned. A group of Quakers, her students, were impressed with the young woman's knowledge and common sense. They brought her patients and supporters. Soon she was able to open a tiny dispensary in the city's worst slum. Later she managed to raise five thousand dollars—enough to finance a forty-bed hospital for one year. In May 1857 the New York Infirmary and College for Women opened. It was staffed entirely by women: Dr. Blackwell, her sister Emily, who had just completed her own medical training, and a European-born midwife, Dr. Marie Zakrzewska, whom Dr. Blackwell had found earning a pitiful living by doing fine embroidery!

By the time the Infirmary was being planned, Dr. Blackwell had gained the support of a small group of men doctors who stood beside her when calamities occurred. The worst was when mobs assaulted the hospital, to take vengeance against the "lady doctors" for a patient who had failed to recover. But Dr. Blackwell kept up her work—in fact, she soon introduced a nurses' training school. In 1865 the hospital's trustees applied to New York State for a college charter to open a medical school, and in 1868 the Women's Infirmary Medical School opened its doors.

Elizabeth Blackwell broke through a barrier, but she did not open the floodgates. The nineteenth-century mind continued to balk at the idea that women be permitted to study anatomy—particularly in the presence of men. Separate medical schools for the sexes provided a way out, and when the University of Michigan finally admitted women to its physician's training courses, it set up duplicate lectures—one classroom for men, another for women—in "subjects likely to create embarrassment"!

By 1890 there were 360 women in America who were

licensed to practice medicine. Though the figure slowly grew, there has never been a sizeable percentage of women physicians. At the present time, fewer than one in ten doctors is a woman. Women today still face many of the problems that traditionally have kept them out of medicine: social pressures that say it is "feminine" to be a nurse but not a doctor; attitudes on the part of vocational counselors and school administrators that direct young women into less "demanding" work; women's own fears that they cannot combine a family and a profession. But even when women succeed in winning the right to practice medicine, they still tend to find themselves clustered in those specialities that are considered "women's domain"—pediatrics, psychiatry, obstetrics, gynecology, anesthesiology—rather than in such "male" fields as surgery, neurology, and internal medicine, which are more prestigious and lucrative.

Part of the reason that women were finally able to become doctors, even in such limited numbers, was that during the nineteenth century, when medicine came to be considered a science instead of a folk practice, such specialties as gynecology and obstetrics were introduced. Women were allowed to "slip in the back door." Although delivering a baby or bringing a sick child to health now required a medical license, it was still close enough to woman's traditional role to be acceptable to society. In other professions, notably law, women headed straight into the storm of controversy about male-female roles.

The Supreme Court of Illinois, denying the application of Mrs. Myra Bradwell to enter the bar in 1870, could not have put the old argument more plainly: "That God designed the sexes to occupy different spheres of action, and that it belonged to men to make, apply and execute the laws, [is] regarded as an almost axiomatic truth." But the decision also indicates something else— that women *had* begun to make progress, and that the court was trying to hold the line: "When the Legislature gave to this court the power of granting licenses," the judges' statement continues,

> it was not with the slightest expectation that this privilege would be extended equally to men and women. . . . This step, if taken by us, would mean that in the opinion of this tribunal, every civil office in this State may be filled by women—that it is in harmony with the spirit of our Constitution and laws that women should be made governors, judges and sheriffs. This we are not yet prepared to hold.

Prepared or not, the Illinois Supreme Court was finally forced to admit Mrs. Bradwell. Not one to give up easily, she had taken her fight to the United States Supreme Court, basing her case on the Fourteenth Amendment of the Constitution and Article Four, Section Two which says: "The citizens of each State shall be entitled to all privileges and immunities of citizens in the several States." The Supreme Court, too, had rejected her plea, on the grounds that citizenship did not in itself confer the right to practice law, which a state may deny. But Mrs. Bradwell had forced the issue, and soon the Illinois legislature stepped into the controversy by passing the most advanced laws of the time, guaranteeing that "no person shall be precluded or debarred from any occupation, profession, or employment (except military) on account of sex."

By the time the Illinois Bar was forced to admit Mrs. Bradwell, women were already practicing law in several other states. In 1879 Belva Lockwood became the first woman lawyer granted the privilege of serving as counsel before the United States Supreme Court.

Slowly but surely the doors of universities and law schools opened to women. Not long after the turn of the century, women attorneys established their own organization, the National Association of Women Lawyers. During this century the number of women lawyers has shown only the smallest gains, rising from 1 percent of the total number of persons practicing law in 1910 to 3.5 percent in 1960. The major breakthrough has just begun. Although at the present time more than 90 percent of the practicing attorneys in America are male, there has been an influx of women into law schools in recent years, with some law schools showing a nearly even division of men and women students. As these new young lawyers enter the field, the statistics will begin to alter in favor of women.

Law, like medicine, remains a field of specialists, and just as in medicine, women tend to find themselves in the areas that duplicate "woman's work" at home. For example, in a listing of the principal committees and members of the New York County Lawyers' Association in 1968, women were members of fourteen of the association's thirty-seven committees. In only four instances were there more than two women on a committee, and the names of the committees show clearly where women attorneys' heaviest participation lies: Children and Youth and the Courts (5 of 16 members); Law, Psychology and Psychiatry (8 of 16); Family Court (6 of 16); and Surrogate Court (3 of 23). There are few women in corporation or international law; women lawyers regularly find themselves working behind the scenes, doing briefing and appellate work rather than dealing with businesses or the public.

Women ministers, doctors, and lawyers have made a place for themselves in fields that have been traditionally all male. What of the "new" professions—engineering, science, accounting—in which age-old prejudices which called women too "modest" for medicine, or decreed that it was God who decided that it "belonged to men to make, apply and execute the laws," were not appropriate? Oddly, as each new profession became a part of modern vocational life, ancient stereotypes were dusted off and refurbished for modern use!

Women in the sciences faced the same difficulties in education and vocational placement as women physicians, and even, having overcome the hurdles to obtaining training, found themselves again in specialties that were in line with "women's natural abilities." Physics, engineering, and accounting require mathematical ability. Despite recent evidence, such as a definitive report, "Mathematics and Sex," by University of California Professor John Ernest, that show that there are no innate differences between the sexes regarding facility in mathematics, women have been traditionally steered by vocational-guidance experts, teachers, and public opinion away from the study of higher mathematics. As a result, fewer than ten percent of all accountants are women, only three out of a hundred engineers are women, and when women enter the sciences they are generally found in biology rather than the physical sciences.

Once again, in line with what is "acceptable" for women, since government service has been open to women since the Civil War, today's woman professional is far more likely to take the Civil Service examination than her male counterpart is. Then too, women seek the assurance that qualifying examinations provide them with an equal chance, whereas they may have to face subtle or even blatant discrimination in private industry. Hence, only 17 percent of all male engineers are Civil Service employees, while more than one in three of all women engineers work in that capacity.

The gap between men and women in the professions has narrowed considerably during the past decade. But more than three centuries after Anne Hutchinson defended her interpretation of the ministry before the Massachusetts Bay Colony courts, and more than a century after the first American women physicians and lawyers asserted their rights to practice, the professions remain heavily weighted in favor of men. How well this generation of young Americans can pierce the barriers of prejudice and tradition remains to be seen.

9

Women in the Arts

Women's entry into the professions was blocked by old myths. Women were "too frail" for the rigors of study. Their intellects were unsuited to higher learning. The work itself would "coarsen" their "natural delicacy of feeling." None of these objections could apply to the arts. Yet listen to Anne Bradstreet describe the prejudice she encountered as a woman poet in Colonial America:

> *I am obnoxious to each carping tongue*
> *Who says my hand a needle better fits,*
> *A poet's pen all scorn I should thus wrong,*
> *For such despite they cast on female wits:*
> *If what I do prove well, it won't advance,*
> *They'll say it's stol'n, or else it was by chance.*

Although Anne Bradstreet railed against the stereotype that required her to mask her talents, her resentment did not prevent her from carrying out all her responsibilities as the hardworking wife of a Colonial farmer. Like other women in the Massachusetts Bay Colony, she had emigrated from England to face the privations of frontier life. Her husband owned a small farm, and Anne worked from dawn to dark helping with farm chores, preparing food, making clothing for their family of eight children. It was not until late at night when the children were sleeping that Anne would light a candle and, with a quill pen and homemade ink, write a few lines. Somehow her genius overcame the odds—the never ceasing labor that brought her, finally, to death before she reached middle age, and most of all the disdain she faced as a "female" who dared to consider herself a writer. Her legacy, a body of graceful lyric poetry, established her as America's first important poet.

Phillis Wheatley faced even harder trials in her search to express her talents as a writer. She was captured in West African Senegal by slave traders in 1761, put in chains, transported in the hold of a slave ship to Boston. There, a shivering, ragged little six-year-old, she was sold to John Wheatley to work as a servant to his wife and children.

The Wheatleys were unusual people. Although it was customary to keep slaves ignorant and illiterate, lest they "get ideas" about freedom, Phillis' owners recognized her shimmering intelligence almost immediately. They taught her to read and write, gave her lessons in astronomy and Latin, and when she demonstrated her abilities as a poet, they became her patrons. They freed her but allowed her to live in their home.

For a time Phillis Wheatley seemed to have overcome the prejudices against her. If a *white* woman was supposed to be incapable of intellectual and creative accomplishment, how much less likely was it that a *black* woman could distinguish herself? Yet Phillis wrote nineteen volumes of well-acclaimed verse. Her "Ode to General Washington" was praised by the first President himself. Her fame spread, and after the Revolutionary War she journeyed to England, where she was feted by literary society.

It was all not to last long. Her patrons died; the man she married was lazy and dishonest and left her destitute with three children. In the winter of 1784, when she was thirty-one years old, she died with her newborn child in her arms, in an unheated Boston rooming house, of cold and starvation. Despite her gifts, there was not yet a place in the world for Phillis Wheatley.

Like all artists, Anne Bradstreet and Phillis Wheatley used the raw material of their own experiences, feelings, and observations. They wrote about themselves, as women living in an era when the life of the mind and imagination were male domains. But they also wrote about the American experience, and the fact is that in the early days of the New World, art and artists were generally held in low esteem. In a practical period of strenuous colonizing, art was considered frivolous. Visual artists channeled their talents into practical forms: beautiful quilts which pleased the eye, but also were used as bedcovers in unheated Colonial rooms; primitive portraits that served as genealogical records for one's children and grandchildren, much like notations in family Bibles. There was no sculpture, and music was restricted to composing hymns to be sung in church. Puritan society called drama and fiction "the powers of darkness," which meant they led people to the devil rather than to God. Whatever writing there was was practical and utilitarian, and although a body of literature came out of the Revolutionary War—including the plays, pamphlets, and verse of Mercy Otis Warren, a well-connected New Englander whose friends included the Washingtons and Adamses—it was not until the early nineteenth century that American art began to flower.

American literature was shaped by the history of the country. For the first century and a half, America was only a group of colonies scattered along the Eastern Seaboard. After the Revolutionary War, it cut its ties with Europe and became a nation. By the end of the nineteenth century the country extended southward to the Gulf of Mexico, north to the forty-ninth parallel, and westward to the Pacific. At the turn of the twentieth century, America had taken its place among the powers of the world. Meanwhile, the rise of science and industry, the birth of the social sciences such as psychology and sociology, changed the way people thought and felt, too. All these had an effect on literature—and art in general.

Following the path of American civilization from the Atlantic to the Pacific, American literature began on the East Coast. In Boston there were the Brahmins, a group of lofty, intellectual New England writers that included James Russell Lowell, Henry Wadsworth Longfellow, and Oliver Wendell Holmes. They were mainly associated with Harvard University—whose doors were firmly closed to women. But a village not far away, Concord, Massachusetts, gave rise to another movement, the transcendentalists. Individualists, reformers, filled with the fiery hope of freeing mankind from the ties of authoritarianism in religion and government, the Concord group experimented with anarchistic and socialistic schemes for living, and believed in woman suffrage, better conditions for workers, and the abolition of slavery. From their ranks came such writers as Ralph Waldo Emerson, Henry David Thoreau, and a "brilliant bluestocking" named Margaret Fuller.

Margaret Fuller's father was committed to the idea of women's equality. At six she was instructed in Latin; by the time she was ten she was reading Shakespeare and Cervantes—and other classics of literature in six languages. Although there was no college that would accept a woman, she pursued her scholarly interests at home until she became both admired and feared for her learning.

Margaret Fuller's first job was teaching at an experimental school in Boston, headed by a well-known transcendentalist named Bronson Alcott. There were even more luminous figures in Margaret's world—Ralph Waldo Emerson, for one. Among them, Margaret—already at work on her first book, a translation of a biography of the German poet Goethe—was considered a brilliant thinker and a gifted talker. When the "heretical" school went bankrupt, her friends encouraged her to begin a series of paid lectures and group discussions for women.

Margaret Fuller's "conversations" attracted the best-educated and most serious women in Boston. More than that, they provided her with an outlet for her ideas about woman's role, and gave her material for the book which was to earn her Susan B. Anthony's accolade: "She possessed more influence upon the thought of American women than any woman previous to her time."

Her *Woman in the Nineteenth Century* is a slim volume, and today it seems quaint and flowery. But its message was radical: Women had a right to higher education; to "grow . . . discern, to live freely and unimpeded." They had rights to whatever work they were fitted to do. "If you ask me, what offices they may fill, I reply—any. . . . Let them be sea-captains, if you will." Most of all, they had rights to "every path laid open to Woman as freely as to Man . . . a *right*, not yielded as a concession."

Margaret Fuller achieved an astonishing number of "firsts." At Ralph Waldo Emerson's invitation she became the first woman editor of *The Dial*, a transcendentalist journal of major literary and political importance. There her work dealt with the issues of the times—abolition; labor exploitation; fair treatment of Indians; changes in marriage laws; prison, hospital, and educational reform. From *The Dial*, she moved on to become the first woman columnist of Horace Greeley's New York newspaper, the *Tribune*. Her literary criticism was considered on a par with that of her rival, Edgar Allan Poe. And finally, she was the first woman to be sent abroad as a correspondent for an American newspaper.

Margaret Fuller's brilliant career came to a terrible and ironic end. All her life she had feared water; at forty, on her way back from Italy (where she had played a major part in the Italian Revolution of 1848) with her new husband and infant child, she was drowned in a shipwreck less than a hundred yards from Long Island's shores. But her work survived her, at least through the century she described; and more than that, her courageous refusal to cut her talents to fit the cloth of custom was a beacon to other ambitious and gifted women of her time.

One of these women, Louisa May Alcott (the daughter of Fuller's first employer, Bronson Alcott), achieved a lasting place in American literature. The second daughter of the dreamy, idealistic reformer was early marked as the support of her family. Bronson Alcott's life was devoted to plain living and high thinking. He experimented in communal living, voluntary poverty, vegetarianism, and mysticism. It fell upon Louisa's thin shoulders to provide the bread and butter for their family of six. From the age of eleven, when her mother called her "my industrious daughter . . . on whom we all depend," it was Louisa's ambition to pay off the family debts and keep the family secure.

Bronson Alcott's friends, Thoreau, Emerson, Nathaniel Hawthorne, and the eminent Unitarian preacher and abolitionist Theodore Parker, all had suggestions about how Louisa could earn her family's keep. They thought she might be a servant, a seamstress, or a teacher. Dutiful Louisa followed Emerson's advice and started a school when she was sixteen. Her first collection, *Flower Fables*, published in 1854 when she was twenty-two, consisted of stories she had told Emerson's children.

The Civil War released Louisa May Alcott—temporarily—from the confines of her loving, dependent family. She volunteered to nurse Union soldiers. Although the experience broke her health—she was never again really well—it gave her the material for the first book to show her real talent: *Hospital Sketches*, published during the middle of the war.

While the book remains—along with the poetry of

Walt Whitman, her contemporary—the most vivid and believable account of the Civil War, it earned its writer only a few dollars. Ailing but obedient to her family's needs, Louisa took a job as companion to an invalid.

It is incredible that in the midst of all her tragedies—her mother and sister died, and then her brother-in-law, leaving Louisa with the care of two young nephews—she was able to write at all. But neither Louisa's almost fanatical devotion, nor her down-to-earth practicality, keen observer's eye, or sharp sense of humor failed her. *Little Women*, a classic in literature, paid off the family's debts and put a nest egg in the bank. Her subsequent books, which include *An Old-Fashioned Girl*, *Rose in Bloom*, and *Little Men*, brought the financial success and acclaim she deserved. Long after Louisa May Alcott's death her books remain popular, and generation after generation of children continue to read them, while the public at large enjoys her work in media the author never dreamed of—radio, television, and motion pictures.

Louisa May Alcott chronicled the Civil War and the postwar period in a way that revolutionized children's literature. Unlike the flowery, preachy pap of the day, her work dealt with real people in real situations. But although her grasp of her society was profound, her political influence was slight. It remained for another daughter of New England, Harriet Beecher Stowe, to write *Uncle Tom's Cabin*, about the most important political and moral issue of her time—slavery.

Harriet Beecher Stowe was born into one of the most remarkable families of the nineteenth century, and the rigid limits that were placed on women of her time rested only lightly on Harriet. Her father, Lyman Beecher, an important influence in American religious thought, was called "the father of more brains than any other man in America." Seven of his thirteen children were prominent in their day, and two—Harriet and Henry Ward—achieved lasting fame.

Harriet's idol was her eldest sister, Catharine, who herself became a leader in the women's education movement. The girls' mother died when Harriet was four, and Catharine raised the younger children. When her sister opened a seminary for girls in Hartford, Connecticut, in 1824, thirteen-year-old Harriet became a student, and then, at sixteen, a teacher.

In 1832, Lyman Beecher was offered the presidency of newly founded Lane Theological Seminary, and the family went with him to Cincinnati, Ohio. Catharine lost no time in establishing a pioneer college for women, The Western Female Institute. While Catharine raised funds and served as the school's administrator, Harriet put her ideas and energy into stories and journals. She wrote for the school magazine, for local publications. Then, a few years after she married Calvin Stowe, a professor at Lane, she published her first book, a little volume called *The May Flower*.

Cincinnati had brought her to a world she had only read about in New England. The Ohio city was a stop on the Underground Railroad—that network of abolitionists, Quakers, and freedom-loving citizens who helped fugitive slaves escape from bondage into the free North and Canada. The city was separated only by the Ohio River from slaveholding communities, and Harriet saw black women making the dangerous journey, sometimes giving up their lives rather than return to plantation slavery.

The eighteen years she spent in Cincinnati formed Harriet's life work. Her husband was elected to a professorship at Bowdoin College, in Brunswick, Maine, and although his family followed him there, Harriet found her thoughts constantly returning to all she had seen and heard in Ohio. She asked the editors at *The National Era*, an antislavery paper published in Washington, D.C., whether they would like a story about slavery. The answer, "yes," brought forth, in serial form, *Uncle Tom's Cabin*.

Uncle Tom's Cabin laid to rest any conscience-saving thoughts Americans might have had about contented "darkies" happily singing spirituals in the cotton fields. The book describes sadistic overseers, indifferent slave masters, the struggle-to-the-death flight of blacks to escape a life of bondage. The book created an instant furor; Harriet was lionized in the North and, particularly, in Europe, damned and burned in effigy in the South. When her book was mocked as being merely the flight of an overexcited imagination, she promptly wrote another: *A Key to Uncle Tom's Cabin*, in which she presented a large number of documents and testimonies to show that, indeed, her description, tragic as it was, was no more than the simple truth.

No serious historian of the Civil War has failed to credit Harriet Beecher Stowe for playing a large part in inflaming public opinion against slavery. She is still considered a name to be reckoned with in summing up the causes of the Civil War. Her later books and essays, too, dealt with the social and political issues of her time, and established a secure reputation for her. No writer, perhaps, has ever more justified the belief that "the pen is mightier than the sword" than the woman whose book helped to change American history.

The plight of blacks became real to Harriet Beecher Stowe's readers, who saw slaves laboring under the whip of Simon Legree; submitting, bowing, and scraping to avoid punishment; and rebelling by fleeing in the night. Another writer, Lydia Maria Child, made her readers see still another group of people who suffered from discrimination—Native Americans.

Like other exceptional women of her day, Lydia Maria Child sometimes despaired of having the time, energy, and courage to accomplish everything she wanted to do. There were so many important causes! Her life encompassed almost all of the nineteenth century—she was born in 1802 in Medford, Massachusetts, and lived until 1880. She saw the beginnings of industrialism, the entrance of women into the labor force, the birth of the women's rights movement, slavery, abolition, the Civil War, the establishment of widespread free education, Reconstruction, and "the Gilded Age"—the rise of monopoly capitalism in which huge fortunes were made by a few at the cost of misery to the vast majority.

There was hardly any humanistic cause which Mrs. Child did not pioneer. She was an activist in the abolitionist movement, working with the Grimké sisters to present the Massachusetts state legislature with petitions opposing slavery. She was a force in the women's movement, protesting that "womankind [were] made chattels personal from the beginning of time . . . insulted by literature, law, and custom." Her books *Hobomok*, *The Rebels*, and *Philothea* defended those who had few others to speak for them—slaves, freedmen, and Indians. At a time when Native Americans were treated with scorn, considered "murderous savages," Lydia Child described her characters with sympathy and respect.

The writer-as-reformer became an increasingly important figure in American literature at the end of the nineteenth century. A great body of literature flourished between the Civil War and 1914—literature of social revolt. The names of these writers glow in American letters—Mark Twain, Edward Bellamy, William Dean Howells. Among their descendants were the "muckrakers"—a name applied by Theodore Roosevelt to describe a group of crusaders who exposed the cruel conditions of life among the working men and women, in order to bring about change in law and public opinion. There was Lincoln Steffens, author of *The Shame of the Cities*, a vivid portrayal of the urban poor. There was Upton Sinclair, whose book *The Jungle*, a description of the filth and brutality in Chicago's meat-slaughtering industry, shocked the nation. And there was Ida Tarbell, perhaps the most influential of all the muckrakers.

Ida Tarbell's most significant work was a book called *The History of the Standard Oil Company*, published in 1904. A carefully researched document, it outlined the ways in which a small group of ruthless men garnered the energy resources of America and turned them into a source of private wealth. The book spurred action by the Federal government to "trust bust"—to break up the giant corporations that were illegal under the Sherman Antitrust Acts. Nearly three quarters of a century later it remains a clear analysis of a question that America still has not answered: whether the natural resources of the country belong to the businessmen who develop them under a system of private enterprise, or to all of the people, whose labor also contributes to American progress and prosperity.

By the end of the nineteenth century, women had earned the right to be taken seriously as writers. Since then, each new movement in American letters has had its share of women interpreters.

Emily Dickinson was too withdrawn from the world to think of herself as being in the mainstream of American literature. Indeed, except for a brief visit to Washington, D.C., and another to Boston, she never went farther from home than eight miles; most of her life was spent behind the sheltering hedges of her own house in Amherst, Massachusetts. Her poetry was not even published under her own name until 1890, four years after her death. Yet the cryptic, sometimes mystical little verses she wrote in her hen-scratch handwriting and kept in bureau drawers and old trunks have influenced generations of poets. Her reputation has grown with the years; today she is considered second only to Walt Whitman in her effect on American poetry.

Poetry, so long condemned by Puritan and frontier society as frivolous and immoral, gradually gained acceptance as a major art form in America. Women poets—as much as men—recorded their time and place in the imagery of poetry. The changing morality after World War I was described by Sara Teasdale and by Edna St. Vincent Millay, whose lyric "My candle burns at both ends" captured the essence of newly freed women in the "roaring twenties."

Other women poets (white and black) defined life as

they saw it. Today's women poets continue to "bind together by passion and knowledge the vast empire of human society"—the very definition of a poet, according to William Wordsworth.

In fiction, too, women gradually gained acceptance as serious novelists. Recognition for an American woman writer came first in this country when Edith Wharton was awarded the Pulitzer Prize for *The Age of Innocence* in 1920, and worldwide in 1938 when Pearl Buck won the highest accolade given to authors, the coveted Nobel Prize for literature.

While women writers progressed from Anne Bradstreet's half-defiant, half-apologetic "versifying" to recognition for a body of work fully as distinguished as that of male writers, women in two other areas of the creative arts—fine art and music—have had a rougher path to tread. The problem has partly been in traditional evaluations of women's abilities, and partly in what has been considered "woman's place." Writing is a "feminine" skill, for women have always been allowed to be verbal, and besides, writing can be done in the protected environment of one's own home. Music, on the other hand, is basically mathematical and abstract, involving areas of abilities in which women are supposed to be disadvantaged. Painting as a vocation challenged even more basic prejudices. While young women were allowed to dabble in watercolors and decorate china, they needed to be protected from the "bohemian" world of painting, with its connotations of sordid studios, wild goings-on with artists' models, and other symbols of sexual immorality. Yet, in spite of almost insurmountable difficulties in being accepted for training in conservatories and art academies, in receiving commissions from universities, civic groups, the government, for symphonic composition, and from galleries and agents who represent artists, women composers and painters have sought to express their talents and satisfy the artist's need for recognition.

How careful the early women musicians had to be not to offend "propriety"! Here is the image those pioneers in the arts had to project: "Mrs. Van Hagen," an advertisement in a Colonial newspaper reads,

> respectfully informs the ladies of this city that she intends to teach the theory and practice of music. . . . As motives of delicacy may induce parents to commit the tuition of young ladies . . . to one of their own sex . . . she flatters herself that she shall be indulged with their approbation and the protection of a respectful public."

There is nothing in the advertisement to indicate that Mrs. Van Hagen, "lately of Amsterdam," was a serious musician who, with her husband, Peter, and son, composed ballads and operas that were performed in theaters in Boston!

Carrie Jacobs Bond, too, encountered all the difficulties people in the arts in America must overcome, as well as a whole set of problems reserved for women artists. Born into a musical family in Janesville, Wisconsin, during the Civil War—one of her relatives was John Howard Payne, who wrote "Home, Sweet Home"—Carrie was a child prodigy. She not only played the piano by ear, but had talents in several other arts. Strong-willed and independent, she divorced her first husband—an act that was practically unheard of in her time and place; but remarriage to a physician, Frank L. Bond, brought little happiness. She was shortly widowed, her investments failed, and a severe fall invalided her. Carrie turned to "women's occupations." She rented rooms, painted china, took in sewing—and sold little songs for twenty-five dollars each. At last she realized that if she was to succeed, she would have to publish her music herself; she would have to be not only a composer, but an entrepreneur as well.

The showcase for talent at that time was New York's Steinway Hall. Carrie Bond scraped together all her money and rented the auditorium for a night. She took ads, printed tickets, set up her own publicity. Then, in a dress made out of an old lace curtain, for her meager funds were exhausted, she appeared onstage to launch her new career.

The gamble paid off. Mrs. Bond's popular music captured the country's interest. Her song "I Love You Truly," published in 1901, sold five million copies, and "A Perfect Day" did nearly as well. Best of all, the royalties from her songs enabled her to continue in serious music. Performances at the White House, for Presidents Theodore Roosevelt and Warren Harding, further established her reputation as America's first important woman composer, an honor that was confirmed when in 1941 the Federation of Music Clubs awarded her that title.

In recent years, women composers have succeeded in overcoming some—though not by any means all—of the prejudices that have historically relegated women to dilletante rather than professional standing. Such women as Ethel Glenn Hier and Miriam Gideon have established places for themselves as composers of note, and Louise Talma has been widely recognized as the "Dean of American Women Composers," winning a coveted National Institute of Arts and Letters award and a Guggenheim Fellowship.

The portrait of woman as painter has undergone an evolution, too. As with literature, painting and sculpture in early America were considered European refinements, frivolous, out of keeping with no-nonsense frontier values. Exceptions were made in the case of well-connected, aristocratic women—Jane Stuart, the daughter of George Washington's portrayer, and Sarah Peale, who painted Lafayette and Daniel Webster. While a daughter of the rich, like Mary Cassatt, could—although at heavy cost—study in Europe and become part of an artistic circle that included the best-known artists in the world, the talented daughters of the poor and middle classes are unrecorded in art history. The odds against acceptance in an academy, recognition in any formal institute, were formidable, and to brave a climate so antagonistic to female artists was virtually impossible.

The breakthrough came sometime after the First World War, paralleling a loosening of the tight bonds of sexual morality. Then, too, America began to take its place among the nations of the world, and American artists looked less and less to Europe as a cultural center. Georgia O'Keeffe, America's most prominent woman artist, never even visited Europe until 1953, when she was sixty-six years old. Her themes were drawn from typically native sources: She painted the flowers and trees and mountains of New Mexico, the adobe buildings that were Native Americans' contributions to architectural form.

In the 1950 census, some two million Americans listed as their occupations the title "artist," and about half of these were women. Art academies and schools, once chiefly the province of men, now accept large numbers of women. More significant, perhaps, is the fact that twentieth-century women artists come from a wide variety of social and economic backgrounds, ranging from the poorest working class to the most affluent.

In sculpture, too, American women have overcome the historical resistance that placed the medium outside of woman's realm: the idea that sculpture required physical strength that women did not possess. Contemporary sculptor Louise Nevelson executes architectural constructions from packing crates and pieces of furniture; Marisol Escobar's work shows the massivity and weight that used to be considered a man's expression.

As creative art assumes contemporary forms—graphics, photography, cinema—women increasingly offer their own contributions. An ad in the *British Journal of Photography* at the turn of the century dissociates the career of photography from the supposed drawbacks of other forms of art: "It is an occupation exactly suited to the sex. There are no weights to carry, no arduous strain of mind and body, it is neat and clean." More to the point is that photographers never had to contend with licensing laws and trade unions by which women have been effectively discriminated against, nor did they need entrance into academies that were largely restricted to men. As a result, women artists have firmly established themselves in photography. Such women as Dorothea Lange, whose portraits of rural Americans during the Depression have been called the most honest view of life during that time; Margaret Bourke-White, whose photojournalism during World War II and the Korean War remains the most graphic record of a war-torn world; and portraitists Diane Arbus and Helen Levitt, who depict the grotesque and ordinary in American life, are recognized for the important contributions they have made to a definition of contemporary culture.

While the ascent to the first ranks in the creative arts has been slow but steady, marked with breakthroughs by women of outstanding talent, women in the performing arts have generally experienced less initial opposition. Dance and the theater were not always socially acceptable ways for women to express their talents—until late in the nineteenth century actresses and dancers were viewed suspiciously as "ladies of easy morals." But perhaps because singing and dancing fall into the category of "feminine graces"—as different from the *creation* of a play or opera, which is considered intellectual work—or perhaps because men could *not* sing soprano, be ballerinas, continue in an age of realistic theater to disguise themselves as females, there has historically been a place in America for women in the performing arts.

As early as 1724 the *American Mercury*, a Philadelphia newspaper, advertised an unnamed performer who "Dances Courant and Jigg upon the Roap, which she performs as well as any Dancing Master does it on the

Ground. . . . Dances with Baskits upon her Feet and Iron Fetters upon her Legs." More seriously, the earliest professional theatrical company in America was probably the one developed by William Livingston, who built a theater in Williamsburg, Virginia, in partnership with Charles and Mary Stagg—Mary being America's first leading lady. Later theatrical companies, such as the "Comedians from London," which became the American Company, list women as well as men in leading roles. In dance, too, women were early ballerinas in classical ballet, and innovated American forms of modern dance.

The persistence of women artists has finally allowed them a place in the mainstream. In literature, there is full acceptance of women's gifts. In music, the path is still rocky: Women are still underrepresented in symphonies, face discrimination as conductors, are hardly found at all in prestigious societies such as the National Institute of Arts and Letters.

Today's artist still faces age-old problems. She needs the time and place to develop her talent, a responsive audience capable of constructive criticism, and a peer group for support. To meet those needs women in the past decade have sought to create a personal environment. The Women's Art Building in Los Angeles, for example, provides studio space and cooperative gallery shows; the Feminist Press in Westbury, New York, seeks out unknown women writers of promise as part of its program to provide a positive climate for women in literature. Women's groups such as the National Organization for Women (NOW) have task forces on women and the arts, sponsor art exhibits, contests, journals, awards, and workshops. All of these efforts are part of a movement toward the development of an individual voice for women—a process that has been paralleled in other areas of women's endeavors in recent years.

10

After Suffrage

Long lines of women, dressed in the floppy hats and hobble skirts of the day, stretched outside the House of Representatives on the cold morning of January 10, 1918. Many of them had been there since dawn, hours before Congress was to convene, to vote on the long-awaited Anthony Amendment—worded exactly as Elizabeth Cady Stanton had written more than a half century earlier: "The right of citizens of the United States to vote shall not be denied or abridged by the United States or by any State on account of sex." The measure, which had been defeated by a narrow margin in 1915 was expected, finally, to pass.

At last the historic moment came. In the bedlam of shouts and cheers from the women who packed the galleries, three roll calls and a recapitulation were needed before the outcome was certain: By a vote of 274 to 136, two more than the two-thirds majority needed to pass a Constitutional Amendment, the measure was approved!

Although the celebration was only symbolic (for in

order for an Amendment to the Constitution to be ratified, two thirds of the state legislatures must approve the vote, and this did not take place until August 26, 1920) the day was a climax of more than seventy years of hope, hard work, and agitation. At first it was only a handful of people who supported suffrage for women, but the Nineteenth Amendment's supporters included a cross section of American women, ranging from "women who usually see Fifth Avenue through the polished windows of their limousines," according to a report in the *Baltimore American*, to "pale-faced, thin-bodied girls from the sweltering sweatshops of the East Side."

After the early victories in the West, the suffrage movement had gained momentum. Carrie Chapman Catt campaigned across the country, bringing thousands of women into the ranks. Frances Willard, head of the Women's Christian Temperance Union (WCTU), led her membership from the socially acceptable antiliquor cause into a broad range of activities that included prison reform, public hygiene, and the controversial push for the vote. By 1880 the WCTU—hundreds of thousands of women strong—endorsed suffrage. Finally, with mass public opinion now behind it, the suffrage movement, long split into factional differences, united under the powerful leadership of Harriot Blatch, Elizabeth Cady Stanton's daughter, to bring to the halls of Congress the Amendment that would, once and for all, assure women the rights to full citizenship!

By the time woman suffrage became national law, women had made significant gains. The First World War had ended on November 11, 1918, and among the reasons for the Allies' victory was the prodigious wartime service of American women. As in the time of the Civil War, women were needed to work in the munitions factories, to take over the production of other military and civilian needs, and even to serve at the front, in France. In the decade before the war, one out of five American women over the age of ten worked outside the home for wages, and women were represented in all but a handful of occupations listed by the Census Bureau. When the war came, the figure doubled. More than that, women moved into completely "male" occupations to substitute for the men who enlisted or were drafted into "the war to end wars."

Women took jobs in blast furnaces, at assembly lines that produced high explosives, machine tools, armaments, railway, automobile, and airplane parts. They worked in refineries and foundries; they worked at copper smelting and with acetylene torches. At the front, General John Pershing sent out a call for women telephone operators to run the exchange for the American Expeditionary Force in France, and thousands of brave women answered. Again, as during the Civil War, women served as nurses, and in this more mechanized conflict as ambulance drivers, bringing the wounded from the field to hospitals.

Naturally, when great numbers of women held jobs that had never before been open to them, the question of equal pay for equal work became important. Working women were not concerned with protective legislation—laws that would regulate their hours, prevent their being required to lift heavy weights or work under conditions that presented physical danger. The fact was that they were holding men's jobs, and not receiving men's pay!

In 1918, the last year of the war, the National War Labor Board, responding to pressure by women, directed government contractors to pay women men's wages when they did men's work. The next year Michigan and Montana passed equal-pay laws supposedly applying to all employment. In 1920, Congress created the Women's Bureau of the Department of Labor, set up under the directorship of a woman, Mary Anderson. The Bureau dealt forthrightly with the question of setting working standards for women; it advocated regulations for working conditions for *all* workers rather than attempting to regulate the gender of the worker. And finally, government set standards in its own house: In 1923 the Civil Service Reclassification Act barred discrimination on the basis of sex from government service.

The First World War set into motion a whole range of far-reaching changes which permanently marked the fabric of American life and particularly affected women. Women's employment itself is related not only to the economy, but to a variety of cultural and social factors—such as customs and beliefs about family life and child rearing, the religious atmosphere of the community—which in turn have bearing on sexual morality, manners, and mores. The shock of the war, plunging the world into worldwide barbarism, swept away the innocent ideals of a pioneer society: hard work, thrift, devotion to the wholesome pleasures of the hearth and home. "A whole generation was caught up in the eat-drink-and-be-merry-for-tomorrow-we-die spirit which accompanied the departure of the soldier to the training camps and fighting fronts," wrote historian Frederick Lewis Allen. The American woman became part of a new morality, freed from the tight Victorian shackles that had bound her in the past.

The entrance of America into a war fought on foreign soil and the victory that followed put the country into an internationalist position. America was never again to be the western outpost of Europe; it became a world power in its own right. Young men came back from France impatient with American provincialism, newly sophisticated as a result of seeing other ways of life, bored with the old-fashioned girl, and ready to accept the changes the war had brought to women. American women became "flappers." They "bobbed" their long hair, replaced the modest prewar hobble skirts that had caused them to walk with little, mincing steps with dresses that ended above their knees, used lipstick and rouge—and emerged as emancipated, modern women.

Postwar prosperity coincided with a building and technological boom. Mass production went into high gear. A new point of mechanical and managerial efficiency was reached when Henry Ford perfected the assembly line. With the expansion came a turn toward the consumer market. Commercially prepared canned goods replaced home processing. Women bought vacuum cleaners, electric washing machines, and irons. Housewives learned to telephone their shopping orders, to buy their clothes ready-made.

Single young women were no longer needed at home to help with the housework. For the first time in American history, the majority of middle-class unmarried women went out to earn wages, to fill a variety of clean, respectable jobs newly created by the skyrocketing needs of manufacturing and commerce. Women set their sights higher—entered colleges, took graduate degrees, became professionals. They went into politics, founded businesses. By 1930, for example, nearly one third of all college presidents, professors, and instructors were women—a figure that stands out in sharp relief compared to fewer than one out of a hundred in 1900, and only one in five in 1910.

The halcyon years after the First World War came to an abrupt end with the crash of the stock market in October 1929, bringing the country into financial disaster and offsetting badly the gains that workers—particularly women, always the most vulnerable group—had made. A spiral was set off: Banks failed, businesses could no longer obtain the capitalization they needed to expand, consumers could not afford to buy the products industry made, and plants and factories all over the country cut back or shut down. Within three years more than fourteen million Americans were out of work.

To meet the needs of a nation in which one out of four wage earners was unemployed, the progressive administration of President Franklin Delano Roosevelt set into motion a vast spectrum of governmental programs to aid the needy, provide jobs and training for the unemployed, and establish standards under which those lucky enough to work would not be exploited. The theory was that a flow of money in the hands of consumers was necessary to maintain industrial production. If people were unemployed they could not purchase goods; if there were no buyers, there would not be the expanding market for goods that a capitalist system such as ours requires.

The government focused its sights on those in the population who either had no marketable skills or for whom the economy, in bad times, provided little opportunity to use such talents and training as they possessed. Programs such as the Civilian Conservation Corps (CCC) provided room and board for thousands of young men while setting them to work building roads and reforesting the wilderness. In the spring of 1935 Congress appropriated nearly a billion and a half dollars to establish the Work Projects Administration (WPA). Between 1935 and 1941 an average of 2,100,000 workers were carried on the WPA rolls, earning between fifteen and ninety dollars a month in jobs that ranged from digging sewers to writing travel guides. Younger people were aided through the National Youth Administration (NYA).

Long unemployment lines, homes and farms repossessed by banks because people could not pay their mortgages, soup kitchens for the hungry, all brought home the fact that a comprehensive social-welfare program was needed. There was now clear evidence that Americans could no longer rely solely on hard work and thrift to provide security for themselves and their families. In a technological nation, jobs are dependent upon factors beyond the control of most working people: increasing mechanization, geographical regrouping, inflations, and depressions. While there were a number of programs already in effect—Federal and state workmen's accident compensation, and state and local welfare—

these measures were fragmented and, at best, ignored vast numbers of the neediest. It remained for the Social Security Act of 1935 to set up a reliable program, financed out of the wage earner's salary, with an equal contribution made by the employer, to provide monthly payments for individuals and families when the wage earner is too old or sick to work, or has died.

The first old age, survivors, disability, and health insurance (OASDHI) benefits under the Social Security Act covered only payments to widows and orphans, and applied only to workers in industry and commerce. Most important to working women was that neither farm workers nor domestics were included in the program. Still, the legislation was a step in the right direction, for it established the agency that would gradually evolve into what it is today—a program that consists of nineteen titles, and covers a wide range of needs. That includes health care for nearly all the nation's over-sixty-five population; a guaranteed pension to retired workers; maintenance for widows, orphans, and disabled minor children of deceased workers. Most important to women workers, the program now covers nearly every type of paid employment—including domestic service.

The New Deal, as the Roosevelt administration was called, was generally committed to the concept of equality in employment and welfare benefits. When the National Recovery Administration industry codes were established in the bleak year of 1933, the new Women's Bureau of the Department of Labor seized the opportunity to get equal pay for men and women written into the program. The Walsh-Healy Act of 1936 set regulations for employees on government contracts, making a double standard of wages illegal, as did the Fair Labor Standards Act of 1938.

President Roosevelt himself set a precedent by appointing the first woman cabinet member. Frances Perkins, an emancipated graduate of Mount Holyoke with a background of settlement work and experience in labor disputes in New York's garment center, filled the important post of Secretary of Labor. Working women also had a powerful ally in the President's wife, Eleanor Roosevelt. She had been an ardent suffragist and campaigner for working women's rights. She had worked with groups such as the Women's Trade Union League, the Consumers League, and the Industrial Board of the YWCA. And yet, despite all efforts on the part of government, the Depression years were, at best, a mixed blessing for working women.

The hard times of the thirties put working women in a bind. They needed to work to support themselves or to help provide for families in which the male breadwinner was unemployed, and yet their work was fiercely resented as competitive with men. "When you give a woman a job, you take one away from a man," was the cry. Married women—regardless of how many dependents they had who relied on their wages—were particularly discriminated against. Many married women had to lie about their status, for it was common practice for firms to force women to leave when they married. Industry took advantage of the situation. If women's paychecks were considered only supplementary, why pay women the same wages as men, who supposedly had to support families? Despite the legislation, equal-pay standards were blatantly disregarded. Sometimes dual pay scales—one rate for men, another much lower one for women—were openly posted on factory gates.

In other ways, too, the Depression was particularly hard on women. In families where money was tight, the decision usually would be made to educate only sons. "A man needs an education, trade, or profession," was the reasoning. "A girl will get married and her education will go down the drain." As a result, the Depression meant not only that women found their chances for advancement restricted, but their daughters, as well, would continue to pay a price in terms of job opportunities and salaries.

It was not an effect immediately felt, for the entry of America in 1941 into another world war again created an enormous need for womanpower. Full wartime mobilization meant the end of the Depression. More than sixteen million American men—out of a population of a hundred sixty million—enlisted or were drafted into the armed forces. For a time every able-bodied man between the ages of eighteen and thirty-eight was subject to the draft; thus, almost overnight, the country went from having a surplus of employees to a shortage. Besides, the reserves of men to serve in the armed forces were inadequate; for the first time in American history, women's auxiliaries to the Army and Navy were established, and women as well as men became soldiers, sailors, and marines.

The first women in the armed forces were volunteers. The branch of service they selected was designated as "auxiliary," and their service was, by law, noncombatant. The idea was that women were to fill clerical jobs to release men for the front: For each soldier who carried a gun or crewed a battleship there was someone needed to issue supplies, decode messages, type reports, and provide the labor for a variety of other jobs. By the hundred thousands women volunteered to become part of the WAAC (Women's Army Auxiliary Corps), the WAVES (Women Appointed for Voluntary Emergency Service, a naval auxiliary), the United States Marine Corps Women's Reserve, the Spars (the women's branch of the Coast Guard, from their motto "*Semper paratus*"), and the WAFS (Women's Auxiliary Ferrying Squadron, the Air Force's auxiliary).

At home, the United States Department of Labor reported that "it can hardly be said that any occupation is absolutely unsuitable for the employment of women." Women in industry were entrusted not only with "men's work" as producers of war matériel—munitions, planes, tanks—but with the responsibility for men's lives as well. A new heroine was created: "Rosie the Riveter." The popular image was a young woman dressed in overalls, lunch bucket under her arm, checking into the war plant to put in her day riveting, welding, taking the place of a man at the front. The woman of the 1940's was, of necessity, independent, self-reliant, capable of taking care of herself and others who were dependent upon her.

The wartime years, in general, brought out a feeling of cooperation among people. In the face of a national emergency, differences between capital and labor—that is to say, those who owned the means of production and those who worked for wages—diminished. Unions agreed not to strike during the war and submitted their disputes to the newly created National War Labor Board. When the United Mine Workers Union decided in May 1943 to disregard the agreement, and struck for higher wages, Congress passed the Smith-Connally or War Labor Disputes Act that required unions to wait thirty days before striking and gave the President the right to seize a struck war plant. Most Americans supported antistrike legislation in the belief that labor's sacrifices were required to win the war.

Much of the reason for the goodwill between employer and employee was that most workers were far better off than they had been in nearly twenty years. The American workforce increased from forty-six million to fifty-three million. As many of these workers were employed at overtime, the work week lengthened from an average of forty hours in 1941 to forty-five in 1944; but to compensate for longer hours, gross weekly wages jumped from an average of twenty-five to forty-three dollars. People not only had money to spend, they had money to spare. With industry engaged in producing wartime goods, the consumer products—cars, refrigerators, washing machines, and a host of other appliances—were not being made. Personal incomes were one-third greater than available goods and services, and most of the excess buying power went into bank accounts and purchases of war bonds. At the beginning of the war, 95 percent of the women war workers said they would quit when victory was won, but by the time the war was actually over—in August 1945—two out of three women war workers asked in a national poll wanted permanent jobs!

But whatever working women themselves wanted became irrelevant with the war's end. Men were returning from the war to claim jobs in a booming economy now moving at top efficiency into consumer production. Young people had deferred marrying during the Depression, and then had lost precious years while men were overseas. Now there were plenty of jobs, wages were higher than they had ever been, and there was no need to put off marriage and raising families. The average age at which women married dropped—and by 1950 it was lower than at any other time during the twentieth century. The birthrate reversed; for the first time since the beginning of the century women began to have more children than their mothers had had.

Women began to lose ground in education, in the professions, and as workers in other fields. In 1950 a record 11 percent of the students graduated from medical school were women, but ten years later the figure dropped to 7 percent. Fewer women entered any of the professions—law, science, engineering, and even teaching, long a woman's stronghold. In 1950, for the first time in more than a hundred years, the majority of elementary-school teachers were men, and the percentages of women in other "women's" professions—library and social work—declined significantly. American women were rapidly being relegated to home and hearth.

A few dedicated reformers tried to buck the tide. Congresswoman Helen Gahagan Douglas led a fight to get a Federal Equal Pay Act in 1945 and again in 1948. Although Mrs. Douglas argued that equal pay would benefit *everyone*, men as well as women—for if there were one pay scale employers would not be likely to replace male employees with lower-salaried female wage earners—unions and employers opposed the law as an invasion of free enterprise. Furthermore, Congress itself was in no mood for reforms. The Women's Bureau, the governmental agency that spoke for working women, barely managed to survive under threats of funding cuts during a postwar economy drive. Women lost a hard-fought battle to open military service as a career choice: The WASPs (Women's Airforce Service Pilots) were permanently grounded, and in 1948 Congress arbitrarily limited women to two percent of uniformed military personnel.

Perhaps the position of women in America would have continued according to the trend of the times—young women marrying earlier, having more children, accepting a vision of femininity that required them to be passive, unambitious, serving as helpmates rather than equal partners with men, giving up personal ambitions and seeking protection and security rather than achievement and financial reward—if it had not been for another, totally unexpected outgrowth of World War II. The catalyst that sparked the changes of our day was the anguished cry of another segment of the population whom history had relegated to second-class citizenship—black Americans.

For most blacks during the first half of the twentieth century, life was an accommodation to the hard realities of discrimination and segregation. The gains they had made under Reconstruction, the years following the Civil War, had been turned back. Through law in the South, and custom in the North, blacks were kept separate from whites. In the South blacks attended separate schools, could not vote because of poll taxes and literacy tests designed to keep them disenfranchised, used facilities—water fountains, bathrooms, railroad-station entrances—designated for "colored" in public places. When, during the First World War and the booming twenties, blacks began the "great migration" to the North in search of legal equality and better jobs, they found their lot not much better. Labor unions, fearing competition with whites for industrial jobs, closed their ranks to black workers. Prejudice as well as poverty kept black Americans living in ghettos, excluded from higher education and other means by which white Americans had achieved upward mobility.

The Depression and the start of World War II brought the economic plight of blacks into focus. A. Philip Randolph, a black labor leader, spoke of assembling a hundred thousand blacks to march on Washington to demand employment in defense industries, and President Roosevelt responded by issuing Executive Order 8802, establishing a Fair Employment Practices Committee to prevent antiblack hiring methods. In the armed services, too, changes were taking place. Under combat conditions, segregation broke down. Another executive order, this time by President Harry S. Truman in 1948, ended the segregation of blacks and whites in military service. And finally, the decision in a Supreme Court case, Brown vs. Board of Education of Topeka, Kansas, in 1954, declared once and for all that "segregation is a denial of equal protection of the laws."

A law on the books is one thing; a law in practice is another. To influence public opinion—to direct the hearts and minds of Americans toward enforcement and acceptance of the laws and a commitment to real equality between blacks and whites—the civil rights movement was launched. Under the leadership of Dr. Martin Luther King, Jr., a young black minister, black men and women in Birmingham, Alabama, organized a protest movement that used nonviolent methods, meeting force with songs and prayers and quiet demonstrations.

The civil rights movement set the pattern for the protest movements that followed during the turbulent period of social change in the 1960's. To match the heightened consciousness of blacks peaceably demanding full equality, the government itself was pressed into passing legislation and enforcing the new laws. The Civil Rights Act of 1957 did little more than create a Commission on Civil Rights with investigatory powers in cases when the vote was denied. The 1960 Civil Rights Act went somewhat further. It gave the Justice Department the right to examine the states' voting records to decide whether local communities were using devious methods to keep blacks from voting.

By the summer of 1963 the civil rights movement had brought matters to a climax. President John F. Kennedy decided that the time had come for a sweeping bill that would grant black Americans the rights they had been denied for nearly a century. He outlined broad new measures, stressing strong legal remedies, in his new bill, with an impassioned plea for its passage—"Above all, because it is *right*."

Although President Kennedy never lived to see it, the bill he wanted was indeed passed. It outlawed discrimination in any state program receiving Federal aid. It outlawed racial barriers in employment and in labor union membership. It gave further enforcement powers against discrimination in voting, against segregation in schools, parks, restaurants, libraries—in every place that serves the public. And through a last-ditch effort by a coalition of segregationist representatives to water down the bill's power, it became the most potent legislation on behalf of women since the passage of the amendment that granted women the vote!

The Southern bloc that opposed equal rights for blacks sought to make the bill an object of ridicule. If they added the word "sex" wherever Title VII—the section that applied to employment—appeared, they reasoned, the bill would open such a can of worms that the entire piece of legislation would be unenforceable. Reading aloud a constituent's letter that poked subtle fun at women, Representative Howard W. Smith of Virginia opened the debate.

Representative Emanuel Celler of New York, floor manager for the bill, rose to support the bill *without* the sex provision: "Imagine the upheaval that would result from adoption of blanket language requiring total equality." Citing areas in which he thought women were protected by law—in alimony, military service, custody of children, and most important, "state and local provisions regulating working conditions and hours of employment," Representative Celler raised the question of the "biological differences between the sexes." He was unprepared for the response.

"Women are protected," was the sarcastic rejoinder of New York Representative Katharine St. George.

> They cannot run an elevator late at night and that is when the pay is higher. They cannot serve in

restaurants and cabarets late at night—when the tips are higher—and the load is lighter. But what about the offices, gentlemen, that are cleaned every morning about two or three o'clock . . . does anybody worry about those women?

The Civil Rights Act of 1964—sex amendment and all—became law on July 2, 1964. To enforce it, the Equal Employment Opportunity Commission (EEOC) opened shop. But the battle was not yet won, for during the next two years the commission carefully steered clear of confrontations on women's rights. When state EEOC heads met in Washington in 1966 to clarify some of the problems in applying Title VII, one of the women in the audience was Betty Friedan, an outspoken advocate of women's rights and the author of a bestselling book about women, *The Feminine Mystique.* Friedan had come with two other women to ask that a resolution be passed requesting the government to begin the fight against sexually discriminatory practices. By the time the meeting ended, the three feminists decided that the only way working women would see change would be through a militant women's rights organization that would pressure the government into action!

NOW—the National Organization for Women—as the new group called itself, made the New York office of the EEOC its first target. Unannounced, Betty Friedan walked up to the first desk and dumped on it huge bundles of newspapers wrapped in red tape, emblazoned with: "Title VII has no teeth! EEOC has no guts." The organization staged other demonstrations, too, to call attention to the discrimination women faced in public accommodations, in jobs, in property rights, contractual rights, in schools, in portrayal by the media. More than that, NOW launched a serious research project to get facts and figures, in order to show women just where they stood at the end of the 1960's.

The pattern of discrimination that NOW unearthed was so consistent and overwhelming that its leaders had difficulty deciding which issues were most urgent. Finally, they decided to concentrate on three that would involve the largest number of women: a campaign to revise the abortion laws, on the grounds that women needed control over their own bodies; child-care centers, because private and government facilities for the care of children of working mothers were inadequate; and the most important of all—equal pay for equal work.

The movement caught the imagination of women all over America. Almost at once, other women's liberation groups formed: Women's Equality Action League (WEAL), Redstockings, Radical Lesbians, Feminists in the Arts, National Coalition of American Nuns, Older Women's Liberation—and countless other professional, high-school, and college groups throughout the country. In the spring of 1970 representatives of dozens of groups met and decided to hold a giant rally in New York to focus the attention of the nation on the need for women's equality.

More than ten thousand women answered the call to assemble in Bryant Park on August 26, 1970. There were housewives, high-school and college students, mothers with children. Women marched behind the banners of professional and businesswomen's clubs. There were secretaries, telephone operators, teachers, social workers,

The expansion of industry increased the demand for semi-skilled, low-paid office workers; and women were available to fill the need.

Switchboard operators in the Marshall Field store, 1890's.

Women office workers, c. 1900.

Members of the Women's Auxiliary Typographical Union in
the 1909 Labor Day demonstration in New York City.

Women were among the last group to be organized by a mostly male labor movement that feared women would take *their* jobs.

Women delegates to the 1886 Knights of Labor convention.

The Strike of the 30,000: shirtwaist makers on strike, 1909.

A sweatshop one year later, 1910.

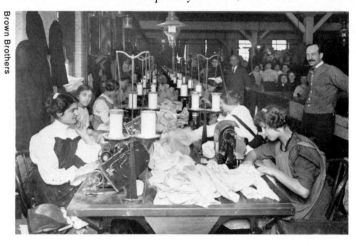

Women and immigrants have always supplied cheap and easy labor to American industry. The Strike of the 30,000 drew attention to conditions which took many more years of struggle to improve.

An early photo of a "secretarial ghetto" at a time when the workers themselves were known as typewriters.

Social work in a New York City settlement house in the early part of the twentieth century, another "service" profession where the concentration of women was high.

A woman mail-truck driver (left) and a woman traffic cop during World War I.

With men at the front, limitations on the kind of work women could do all but disappeared.

Women working in a World War I munitions factory.

Norman Rockwell immortalized "Rosie the Riveter" on a *Saturday Evening Post* cover in 1943 . . . perhaps he was hinting at the fate of women who do men's work.

lawyers, artists. Signs proclaimed the issues of the day: A contingent of college students held a flag that read: "Princeton Grads Take Placement Tests. Vassar Grads Take Typing Tests." Other signs, too, pointed out the differences in job opportunity and advancement, the inequality of pay scales, discrimination in the professions, in organized religion, in higher education.

At the end of the day, bandstands dismantled, bunting folded up and put away, the weary marchers slowly dispersed and went home. Exactly a half century had elapsed since suffrage. Now, after fifty years of sporadic gains and losses, advancement and retreat, American women were once again mobilized in a feminist movement. It was time for women to take on the challenge of the demonstration—to *confront your own unfinished business of equality.*

11

Equal Pay
for Equal Work

Equal pay for equal work.

Of all the demands that working women could make, this one is surely the least controversial. Even the most hidebound conservative could agree that it is only right and fair that women earn no less than men for performing the same jobs. Anything else goes against the basic American sense of justice and fair play.

And yet in 1977, fifteen years after the Equal Pay Act made equality of salary the law of the land; after thousands of affirmative-action cases in which women gathered facts, gave testimony, lawyers wrote briefs, juries deliberated, and judges decided; after a decade of picket lines and demonstrations, strikes and newspaper headlines, American women who work full time earn only $6,000 a year compared to the $11,800 averaged by men, and the gap is actually widening!

A quick rundown of statistics paints the picture.

Among people in professional and technical work—engineers, doctors, teachers, dentists, psychologists, scientists—men earned a median salary of $10,257 a year, according to the United States Department of Commerce's figures for 1970, the year of the last nationwide census, while their female colleagues brought in a median of $6,013. Among managerial workers in industry and commerce there was an even greater gap; men earned twice as much. In occupation after occupation the difference remains consistent: male clerical workers, $7,135; female, $4,124. Taken by percentages, women engaged in crafts earn 52.9 percent of what men do; as farmers and farm managers, only 45 percent; and as farm laborers, only 42 percent. According to economist Dixie Sommers, writing in the *Monthly Labor Review*, men earned more than women in every occupation except public-kindergarten teaching!

There is more to the picture of discrimination than just the differences in salary scales. The kinds of jobs that women are likely to hold are those in which all salaries—for both men and women—are lower than those which are considered "men's work." While industrial production in America began as a "unisex" operation, and it did not matter whether it was a man or a woman who threaded a bobbin or pedaled a shuttle, as industry spread women and children became a source of cheap labor, with the "less arduous" jobs reserved for them. The "feminization" of certain kinds of work meant less pay for all. Today, although the production of goods has increased enormously during the twentieth century, the labor force directly engaged in producing those goods has not. Women have remained concentrated in the same industries that historically have claimed them: garment, textile, tobacco, and other light, nondurable goods. Their work is still likely to consist of making or assembling small items, packaging, labeling, inspecting, machine tending.

Although it takes fewer people to produce more goods, the number of women in the labor force has steadily increased. The largest part of the growth in women's employment has been absorbed by clerical, secretarial, and other office work. Today more than seven million women work as file clerks, typists, stenographers, secretaries, and operate switchboards and computerized office equipment. These positions occupy four out of every ten women who work for pay. Another field in which women workers have been absorbed is retail sales, which accounts for nearly two million women. All together, factory, farm service, clerical, and sales occupations employ about seventeen out of every twenty women in today's labor force, with most of the remainder concentrated in "women's professions"—social work, teaching, nursing, library work.

Statistics give us a general picture of where women are today in their working lives. But behind lists, graphs, and percentages, averages and medians, there is the actuality of millions of women going off each day to be part of the workforce. What the figures show is that a woman today is likely to work in a typing pool, on an assembly line, or at a sewing machine, in a department store or a supermarket, as a waitress, bank teller, motel clerk, telephone operator, insurance-claims file clerk, beautician, or cleaning woman. The jobs are often repetitive, routine, and nearly always dead-end.

Beyond the pay scale there are working conditions—

safety from health hazards, hours, rest periods, overtime work. There is the question of advancement: How far up can a woman go in a job? If she begins as a secretary or trainee, will there be an opportunity for her to move into management, or will the better jobs be somehow designated "For Men Only"? What about fringe benefits such as pensions, disability, health and hospital care? Will she, simply because of her sex, pay higher premiums— have more of her salary deducted—and then realize fewer benefits? What about her old age, the years in which she will have to fall back on savings to replace a paycheck she can no longer earn?

Surveying general employment for women, it becomes clear that the wage scale is only the tip of the iceberg. All of the facets of employment are related—dependent on each other. A woman on the low end of the wage scale is likely to be doing unskilled work; this also means that she is easily replaced—in a "disposable pool." She will be the first to be fired in case of seasonal unemployment, recession, market changes. As a result, women's unemployment rates are three times higher than men's. If she must go from job to job she loses out on company benefits, long-term pension plans, hospitalization. As a result, only two percent of employed women ever realize pension benefits that companies establish privately. Finally, since Social Security benefits are determined by the earned salary over a period of years, the inequities never even out. Women's Social Security benefits are, on an average, lower than men's because they earn less. Broadly speaking, the rewards for a lifetime of lower wages are lower benefits on retirement or during disability.

What is it that has established such a consistently bleak

situation for working women? Part of the answer lies in the economy of the country itself. But that is not the whole story. Three other factors play their parts. First, there is a general mythology about working women, based on a combination of historical stereotypes and prejudices. Secondly, there is the conditioning women receive from childhood—ways of viewing themselves and their capabilities, their aptitudes—in short, what society defines as sex roles. And finally, there are societal conflicts and unresolved accommodations about woman's biological role, for in any society women are the child-bearers and, at least when the children are very young, the child rearers.

To begin with, employers maintain certain beliefs about women as workers, in spite of strong evidence to the contrary. Here are some of the catchphrases:

"Women have greater absenteeism. They are less healthy than men. They have to stay home and take care of other members of the family—children, husbands—who may be ill."

"Women are too emotional for decision-making jobs. They go to pieces under pressure. They are impulsive instead of being reasonable."

"Women are too aggressive when they are in executive jobs. They antagonize other employees." Or, conversely: "Women are not aggressive *enough*. They prefer to take a backseat."

"Men don't like to work under women. For that matter, neither do women—there is too much rivalry."

"Women can't do certain kinds of work. They don't have mathematical abilities. They are not mechanically inclined. They can't lift heavy weights, be useful in any job in which physical strength is required. They can't be firefighters, police officers, for the work is too dangerous."

Over the years a considerable amount of research has gone into examining these beliefs. Every one of them has proved false! For example, the U.S. Presidential Commission's report on women found that as a whole women have two and a half times as much turnover in jobs as men—when the criterion is simply gender. But such comparisons are too broad to be of any real use. When male and female employees are divided into age groups, salary levels, job classifications, there is no difference at all!

Other myths have been exploded, too. The Stanford Research Institute examined absenteeism among women and men. It found out there was a difference—but the study favors *women*: men average 5.4 days a year away from the job, while women are out only 5.3 days. Looking into attitudes about women as executives, studies found that workers who had never had women supervisors held the traditional objections. But surveying groups of workers who had had personal experience with women in positions of authority, more than three quarters of them were satisfied that women were as fair and as competent as men! And finally, the myth that there are inherent sex differences in aptitudes and knowledge between men and women has come under attack. Again, a comprehensive study revealed that of the twenty-two aptitudes tested—language skills, mathematical ability—there were no differences by gender in fourteen, while in those where there were differences, women excelled in six skills, while men were ahead in two!

Although there is no justification in fact for the belief

that women are unsuited for certain kinds of work, the old myths die hard. Even harder to erase are attitudes that society reinforces upon women *themselves*. Perhaps the most illuminating of all studies on this subject was conducted by Dr. Matina Horner in a paper entitled "Why Women Fail."

Dr. Horner's extensive research was done at the University of Michigan. She asked one group of students to write a theme for which she supplied the opening sentence: "After first-term finals, John finds himself at the top of his medical class." Then she selected another group, as similar to the first as she could find, and gave them the same sentence—with one important difference. This time it read, ". . . *Anne* finds herself at the top of her medical class."

The themes were eye-openers. While the vast majority of students—both men and women—wrote admiringly about "John," "Anne" was viewed as a freak! The imaginary "medical student" was described as socially inadequate, a bookworm, an aggressive, ambitious person whom nobody admired—and worst of all, who hated herself! She was made to see the error of her ways for competing as a student, forced to renounce friendship, romance, marriage. The most startling fact about the test was that while neither men nor women approved of "Anne," the most severe criticism came from the women students!

Dr. Horner's research confirmed how effective is the training that supports the double standard—one set of demands, rights, and responsibilities being placed on men, another on women. It is no wonder, for the conditioning begins almost from the moment a baby is born, continues throughout school, is reinforced by the media, ascribed to by psychologists, sociologists—a sometimes subtle but often blatant "brainwashing" directed at young women growing up in America today.

The message begins in the cradle. Boy babies are dressed in blue, girls in pink—a clue for visiting relatives and the world at large about how to act. Girls are cuddled and cooed over; boys are roughhoused. Later, girls are given toys that reinforce their "femininity": nurses' uniforms, miniature housekeeping tools, "bride dolls"; while boys get sports equipment, building blocks. In "Woman's Changing Place: A Look at Sexism," a pamphlet prepared for the Public Affairs Committee, Nancy Doyle describes a scene observed by mothers who organized a sex-roles committee at a private, parent-cooperative school in Brooklyn, New York:

> Beginning in kindergarten . . . the teacher squeezes the child into tight image-molds—sometimes in subtle ways, without even realizing it. A male teacher, for example, told a girl working on a construction set that she hadn't hammered the nails in far enough. Then he said, "I'll do it for you." But when he made the same observation to a boy working on a set, he said, "Hammer the nails down harder." The message is clear: girls are done for, boys strike out on their own.

Then an even more telling tableau:

> Before one little girl dared to venture over to the building blocks section, monopolized by boys, she first fortified herself in a feather boa, twelve

jangling bracelets and several strands of beads, from the costume box. She was letting the world know she wasn't confused about her sexual identity—a mini-version of some women who "make it in a man's world" and feel they must camouflage their success with exaggerated "femininity."

Schools themselves, in their curricula and counseling, continue the message: Girls are frail, noncompetitive, home-oriented. In introducing into the Senate the Women's Equal Education Opportunity Act of 1974, Senator Charles Percy summed it up this way:

> Study after study has exposed sex discrimination at all levels of our educational system. Barriers that confront women on the educational ladder range from female stereotyping in grade school to the exclusion of girls and women from classes and programs designed for men, to the relegation of women to low-paying, low-level positions in schools, colleges and universities.

The results of the role-image conditioning are predictable. Studies show that in the United States fewer gifted women than gifted men even enter college. About half of the brightest 40 percent of high-school graduates go on to college. Of the half that stay away, two thirds are women! Furthermore, it is an uphill battle for women students all the way, and many do not make it. More gifted women than gifted men drop out, according to a study of the National Merit Scholarship Corporation. Not surprisingly, the greatest percentage of women who drop out of college are in the fields that are considered "male"—engineering, business, mathematics.

Once women are out in the business world, the combination of women's own underestimation of their talents, society's negative attitude toward success and
power, and women's limited opportunities takes its toll.
A recent study conducted by women in the publishing
field offers some insight into the way the machinery
operates to place women in lesser positions. Women, for
example, are not told directly that certain positions are
open only to men; what happens is that women are
simply subtly bypassed for promotion. This is also true
in the field of finance and banking, which is by all odds
the most exclusive of women. In order to remedy the
situation, the National Association of Bank Women set
up a foundation in 1975 at Simmons College in Boston, to
finance an academic program for female bank executives.

Simmons College was a natural choice, for the school
has for some time had a graduate program in management
geared for women exclusively. The Simmons professors,
Margaret Hennig and Anne Jardim, have analyzed some
of the problems that women encounter in functioning in
corporations. For example, women tend to overwork and
concentrate on small details rather than delegate responsibility, for they think they will be tolerated only if they
are superefficient. Women are afraid to ask questions
because they fear seeming incompetent, and they are
slow to assert themselves because they might seem pushy.
Then, too, women are excluded from the informal
channels of communication in which men make con-
tacts—business luncheons, "nights out with the boys,"
recreational activities such as golf games and other
country-club sports. Author Caroline Bird, in her book

Born Female, quotes a woman promotion director who paints a graphic picture of the problem: "They go to lunch to tell the men about a change in policy, but they send me memos. When you get a memo, you can't answer back." A highly placed woman executive in a nonprofit organization, who should have been in on board meetings, confessed that she was forced to listen through a ventilator to find out what was being planned at these sessions, from which she was excluded only "because women had never attended."

While women's own conditioning and prejudices on the part of employers play a heavy part in keeping women at the low end of the work ladder, there is a more basic—and as yet unresolved—bind for working women. *Employment standards are geared to the life patterns of men, not women.* A man is expected to work, *and* marry and have a family, but as Charlotte Perkins Gilman pointed out in *Women and Economics*, published in 1898, "All the roles a female is permitted to play derive from her sexual functions." What this means is that neither society's accommodations—arrangements for leaves of absence during pregnancy, guarantee of a job on return to work, child-care facilities for working mothers with preschool children, after-school care for older children of working mothers—nor society's attitudes have yet caught up with the fact that today there are twenty million working wives.

To deal with attitudes first: American men traditionally have been taught to think of themselves as breadwinners. The ability to support a wife and family is considered a mark of success. Many husbands feel threatened when their wives work, either because they see women's labor as competitive or because a working wife announces to the world that a husband does not earn enough. For this reason, working women frequently have to deal with opposition from husbands—expressed either directly or subtly. "We discussed my returning to work," a woman interviewed for an article in *Family Circle* explained.

> My husband agreed. All seemed fine. Would you believe it, on the very first day as I was dressing to go to work, he became completely unglued and spent an hour voicing all the traditional reasons for not having a working wife. I was undermining his masculinity. I was embarrassing him before his friends and family. I was planning to find another, richer husband—the whole grim bit. But I went to work anyway.

There is another hassle. Housework is considered a woman's job. While studies show that husbands of working women *do* take over a slightly larger part of the duties of cooking, cleaning, marketing, and child care than husbands of full-time homemakers do, by and large working women still add an additional thirty to forty hours running a home to their hours as wage earners. This differential is found on *all* levels of women's occupations: A recent study showed that seventy-five percent of women working full time as physicians had no household help, and continued to do almost full-time homemaking as well as medical work.

The strongest conflict that a working woman must face, however, is not around a husband, but when children are involved. Here again is an excerpt from *Family Circle*—a woman who has opted *not* to work puts the problem into a few words: "My 13-year-old . . . told me: 'I like you being here when I come home from school.' Four of our five children are already in school and we have a 9-month-old. But I feel that my 13-year-old needs a mother at home just as much as our baby does."

If, indeed, a woman does manage to cope with her own guilt and overcome the objections of husband and children to her work, she has no easy answers to *how* to provide substitute care for her children. "A job is great," one woman wrote wistfully in response to the *Family Circle* questionnaire, "if you can only afford the baby-sitting." She was not alone. "Many more mothers of preschool children would work," continues the magazine's survey, "if they could afford child care. Nearly one out of seven of our working mothers under 30 says they have been prevented from working at some time for lack of adequate day-care centers in their communities." "These women were not necessarily the poorest—nearly a fourth had incomes over $15,000."

Employers take advantage of the fact that women's priorities are toward their families. Women workers are channeled into part-time work (some 32 percent of all women workers have part-time jobs, as compared with 13 percent of men workers), thus sparing the employer the expenses of paid sick leaves or vacations (and sometimes unemployment insurance), and frequently permitting minimum wage rates. Then, too, part-time work often does not qualify as "work experience" by the standards of most personnel departments, permitting the hiring of women workers at a low salary level.

Most women, of course, are not willing to give up

marriage and a family for a career. The compromise is a split working life. The curve hits its first peak at about age nineteen (when 35 percent of all women work), and its second peak at age fifty (when 49 percent work). Obviously, this means that women, unlike men, have a fifteen- or twenty-year gap in their working lives. Many leave jobs just when they are beginning to advance, and then stay at home—or take part-time jobs—while their children are preschool and school age. When they return to work, they have lost the years in which their men co-workers were steadily climbing up the ladder. The late return to work means that women come back to the job market without rank, skills, or accomplishment, frequently having fallen out of touch with technological, scientific, and business advances. Ironically, at the time most men are at the peak of their career achievement, women are offered unskilled jobs or jobs far below those held by men with similar educational levels.

These patterns are widespread among middle-class, mainly white women. For most minority-group women— some 70 percent of whom are workers, a far greater percentage than among white women—other difficulties block the way. "All women are poor vis-à-vis men," said Aileen Hernandez, an urban-affairs consultant and a former president of NOW, "and the minority woman is by far in the worst economic plight." Minority women have the worst of all possible worlds, Ms. Hernandez points out, because they are often excluded on the basis of race from jobs to which other women have gained access: in clerical, sales, and similar positions. In addition, they are excluded on the basis of sex where minority men have begun to gain access: blue-collar craft jobs, managerial training, law enforcement. Again, these avenues of discrimination show up in income figures, for ranging from top to bottom, the pay scales in America are: white men, minority-group men, white women, minority-group women. Then, too, they show up in the kinds of jobs that minority members hold: a heavy concentration in domestic work, unskilled labor such as restaurant work, in farm work as migrant workers, in factories doing light assembly work.

To see the fruits of years of discrimination is easier than to uproot the plant itself. But individually and collectively, women have been working for the past ten years to improve the lot of working women through four methods: by influencing changes in the social training of women that causes them to accept their own second-class position; expanding social services to make them serve the needs of working women; working through unions and other working-women's organizations to apply pressure on employers; using the laws that the civil rights movement and the women's movement pressed to obtain, and mobilizing women to continue to influence government to take women's priorities seriously.

For the time being the most powerful, pragmatic answer is the law. Here is a rundown on Federal legislation enacted since 1963—what its provisions are, and how it works for women in the labor force:

The *Equal Pay Act of 1963* is the first sweeping Federal legislation in the field. It is unequivocal and, unlike some of the other remedies, it is enforceable too. The law says simply that if a woman can prove that men are being paid more for doing a job that entails the same effort, skill, and responsibility as she is putting forth, she can notify the Administrator of the Wage and Hour Division of the Department of Labor in Washington.

If the complaint is well founded, the agency has the power to order an employer to pay back wages for the period during which the wages were discriminatory. This legislation has another important feature: It provides for complaints to be made anonymously, which means that if a woman is afraid that her employer will punish her, one way or another, for making a complaint, she does not have to attach her name to a document. Since 1963 more than $37.5 million has been found due to 91,661 employees, almost all of them women.

Executive Order 11256, as amended by 11374, is a Presidential order. It prohibits discrimination by an employer who has a contract or subcontract with the Federal government. Under this order the government can withhold payment until the employer or institution gives proof that it has stopped discriminating. While this order, unlike legislation passed by Congress, does not have the force of law behind it, which means that a discriminatory employer cannot be sued, it controls the purse strings and therefore has a lot of clout. It has been particularly useful to women at universities holding Federal contracts for research and development projects. In these institutions, the percentages of women who hold jobs above the lowest levels—visiting lecturer, lecturer, for example—or who are tenured are often far below the number of capable women available.

To set standards for this order, the Office of Federal Contract Compliance issues guidelines. The OFCC designates the Department of Health, Education, and Welfare (HEW) to oversee compliance in education, while the Department of Defense regulates contracts in industry. Women in universities again have been active in using this order; they have organized research committees, prepared papers showing the dollars and cents of discrimination, and volunteered for interviews.

Executive Order 11478 extends Executive Order 11256 into the legislative and judicial branches of the Federal government and also holds sway over the government of the District of Columbia. It is administered by the Civil Service Commission.

By far the most important single piece of legislation enacted on behalf of working women is the history-making *Title VII* of the *Civil Rights Act of 1964*. What Title VII says is simply this: No employer, employment agency, or labor union can discriminate in any aspect of employment on the basis of "race, color, religion, sex, or national origin." Complaints in every area except the four that are not covered by the bill—government employees, teachers and other employees of educational institutions, law enforcement agencies such as the police, and the military—are investigated by the Equal Employment Opportunity Commission. Unlike the Equal Pay Act of 1963, this law does not provide for anonymous complaints, but there is another potent feature: A woman can file a complaint individually, or she can join with a group acting on behalf of all those female employees to whom the discrimination applies. This is known as a "class action"—and it has proved to be the most successful kind of sisterhood suit.

Women pressing affirmative-action suits with the Equal

Employment Opportunity Commission have taken on the most formidable of employers. Highest on the list was one of the giant employers of women, the American Telephone and Telegraph Company. The result of the suit in 1973 was that the corporation agreed to give twenty-eight million dollars in raises and seventeen million dollars in back pay to women of all races and minority men—the largest single settlement in history!

In June 1974 the Bank of America, the largest commercial bank in the world, hard pressed in a successful class-action suit by its female employees, agreed to establish a $3.75 million trust fund exclusively for women—to be used for advanced training, education, sabbatical leaves, and other steps toward career development. In addition, the bank agreed that until 1980, women would constitute 45 percent of all candidates for its officer-training program.

Federal legislation has opened the way for the elimination of subtle ways that have preserved job bias. For example, employers can no longer advertise under help-wanted columns headed "Male" or "Female." Employment agencies can be sued for sending men out early in the morning to apply for positions while saving afternoon interviews for women. It is illegal to refuse to hire or to dismiss an unmarried mother as long as a company retains unwed fathers! Bread-and-butter issues, too, are part of Federal legislation: Sick leaves, vacations, insurance, and pensions must be the same for both sexes. Job classifications no longer hold up by gender distinction: Part of the A T & T settlement was an agreement to place women in traditionally male-held craft jobs—the better-paying work of installation, repair, and maintenance—and men in clerical jobs as typists and switchboard operators.

As women come together to fight job bias, they increasingly look to innovative ways of dealing with less obvious forms of discrimination. For example, men are frequently recruited for higher-paid work by word of mouth—a businessmen's informal "buddy system." To fight this, some university groups publish "blacklists" of sexist employers, and have staged strikes to keep those companies' recruiters away from campuses. Women's political caucuses, women's coalitions in such industries as publishing, professional alliances such as Women in Banking, all are ways of taking informal class action to promote the cause of working women.

Unions, too, serve a purpose. In 1970 union women who worked full time earned $452 a year more than nonunion women. But only one working woman in seven today belongs to a union, and within them women occupy only four percent of leadership positions.

In the winter of 1974, some three thousand women members representing fifty-eight labor unions banded together to form the Coalition of Labor Union Women. The Coalition's purpose was not only to encourage unions to organize the vast majority of the nonunionized female labor force and to fight discrimination by employers, but to deal with nitty-gritty issues that our society still has not solved: legislative proposals for adequate child-care facilities, "livable" minimum wages, improved maternity and pension benefits.

Olga Mada of the Coalition and the United Automobile Workers summed up the group's thrust: "When the women's movement started, many union women had the same cultural hangups as the men about women having an equal role. But the women's movement has been helpful in making union women and blue-collar wives aware that there was blatant discrimination against women. . . ."

The "cultural hangups" that prevent women from seeking better jobs and higher wages, and from generally moving toward par with men, are lingering problems. To counteract women's poor role images, feminist groups have formed committees to pressure the media to stop presenting women as "sex objects" or empty-headed domestic slaves. NOW's media committee published a flyer that chided: "You've got a long way to go, baby," and urged women to write letters to television stations to protest certain advertising slogans. The group gave its approval to a pharmaceutical company that published an ad showing a woman physician examining a baby. "Buy the product and write to the advertising company," the flyer directed.

On its most basic level, work must begin with young people in school, the women's movement believes. Toward this end universities and colleges have been setting up women's studies programs. In order to help lobby for the support of women's studies on campuses and in elementary and secondary schools around the country, more than five hundred women from throughout the United States met at the University of San Francisco to found the National Women's Studies Association in 1977. The new organization cited figures: As of 1976, more than a hundred colleges and universities offered majors and minors in this new field, at least a dozen had programs on the master's level, and there were three universities giving Ph.D.'s in feminist studies.

But it is not just on the high-school and college level that reversal of sexist education must begin. Conditioning starts in prekindergarten days, and to deal with change in the images of men and women for this generation, the women's movement has directed efforts toward children just beginning in school. Feminist groups such as NOW have launched educational committees to screen textbooks and to recommend books that portray women in a favorable way. The committee influenced the State Board of Education of California to drop a primer that portrayed "Mother's chief occupation" as "washing dishes, cooking, sewing, ironing, and wearing aprons." Among the books recommended for school libraries is *Mommies at Work*, by Eve Merriam, published in 1969. It shows women in high-status jobs—scientists, lawyers, and business executives.

To turn around the patterns that an economy and culture have established for three hundred years is no easy task. Women today have much going for them— enforceable laws, increasing public awareness of the plight of working women, and most of all, a growing, supportive sisterhood. Like all progressive social movements, the cause of the working woman looks back to draw its lessons from the past—but places its hopes and directs its goals toward the future.

12

Directions for the Future

Something happened!

We are witnessing what Eli Ginzberg, the Chairman of the National Commission for Manpower Policy, calls "the single most outstanding phenomenon of our century."

More than that, he continues, "Its long-term implications are absolutely unchartable. It will affect women, men and children—and the cumulative consequences of that will only be revealed in the 21st and 22nd centuries."

The central figure in this startling evolution is the American working woman. While women have been going into the job market in increasing numbers—five million more during the 1950's, eight million more in the 1960's—the tide has suddenly become a flood. A million women took jobs outside the home in the first half of 1976. The majority of these new workers are between the ages of twenty-four and forty-four—the group that throughout our history has always stayed at home to have children and raise them. Now, nearly half of all women over sixteen work, or want to, and the projection is that the figure will reach 50 percent within the next three years. At the end of 1976 women accounted for more than four out of ten members of the national labor force—a figure that Labor Department forecasters as recently as three years ago did not expect to be reached for nearly another decade!

The broad social revision through which we are now living goes far beyond the strides in American technology which accounted for the growth of the female industrial force in the past. We are seeing changes in the very fabric of American life:

We have become a nation of two-earner families. Rising expectations about the standard of living—three generations of booming consumer production—have put many, if not all, of these on the list of advantages American families expect: a privately owned home; at least one and frequently two cars; appliances such as washing machines, dishwashers, television sets, air conditioners; college educations for the family's children; vacations and possibly a vacation home; attractive clothing; sports and hobby equipment; and a host of other goods and services. To meet these horizons of comfortable living requires that wives' paychecks be added to those of husbands in hundreds of thousands of middle-income families.

Our demography has undergone extensive change. During the 1960's, the number of women between the ages of eighteen and twenty-four rose fifty percent—a result of the "baby boom" after the Second World War. These women now represent the largest increase in the working population. Death rates among women have altered drastically. While at the turn of the century men outlived women, and as recently as 1920 there was only a year's difference in male and female mortality rates, advances in contraception and a lower death rate in childbirth mean that on an average, today's woman can expect to outlive a man born at the same time by nearly eight years. There are presently ten million widows in America and the figure is expected to grow.

Family patterns have altered radically. American women are marrying later or not at all, are getting divorced and separated at a previously unheard-of rate, are having fewer children or none at all. Among women who are now between thirty and thirty-four years old, more than half married during their teens. But today's young woman—aged twenty or twenty-one—is likely to be single, with only forty out of a hundred married. The divorce rate is now one divorce for every four marriages. A century ago the average woman had eight children. Today she has 2.7, and among women in their twenties, fewer than two. For the first time in history, the nation has a falling birthrate. In one major city, Washington, D.C., there were more abortions than live births in 1976; in another, New York City, there were four live births for every three abortions.

Childbearing and child rearing no longer occupy the better part of a woman's life. Fifty years ago her last child left home when the mother was fifty-six years old. Today the average woman is through with childbearing at age twenty-six; in her mid-forties she is unlikely to have any children living at home. While recent projections indicate that younger women are choosing to postpone childbearing, smaller families and a greater life expectancy combine to insure that most women will have more than half their adult lives before them after their childbearing and child rearing years end.

America is in the throes of the longest period of spiraling inflation in its history. The close of 1976 marked the twenty-second consecutive year in which the cost of living had risen, the first time in which there has been such a long period with no leveling-off or reversal of the trend. For a nonfarm family in a Northeastern city, the poverty cutoff at the beginning of 1977 was ten thousand dollars a year for a family of four. Women, who in the past were not required to bring home wages to supplement the income of the main breadwinner—the husband—now have had to take either part-time or full-time jobs.

Advances in medical science, lowering of maternal mortality rates, and the widespread use of contraception have placed a pool of women in the workforce. A lengthening life span because of antibiotics and other medical breakthroughs means not only that women live longer, but also that they enjoy better health and vitality throughout their lifetimes. More important, perhaps, is the general availability of effective birth-control methods. Women can decide to have children or not, can plan when they wish to have them; more than that, with the elimination of the heaviest penalty a woman had to pay for sexual activity—unwanted pregnancy—there also has been a general relaxation of rigid morality taboos. A general climate of sexual freedom has been created. Not long ago a young woman who entertained a man without a chaperone was suspect. Today's unmarried women are increasingly free to live and work away from home, to travel, to attend out-of-town business conventions with male colleagues, without shocking society. While this new permissiveness is part of a process that began with the "jazz-age flapper" of the twenties, it has just recently come into full flower.

Interwoven with patterns of demography, scientific know-how, and economic factors are more subtle strands that are creating the broad social changes we now see. There are social and political movements—the civil rights movement that set the stage for realization of the American ideal: the concept that *all* Americans are to be afforded equal rights and equal opportunities. More direct in its effect on women is the civil rights movement's legacy—the women's liberation movement.

The women's movement that began in the 1960's made women's career aspirations respectable. Outstanding women educators, writers, and others in public life came forward to encourage their sisters to seek self-expression outside the home, to set loftier goals, to go on to college and graduate schools, and even to penetrate such male bastions as medicine and the law. The psychological climate induced by publicity over the women's movement made it socially acceptable for young mothers to work. It encouraged older women to return to the job market. It sparked Federal laws that increased hiring opportunities and a burgeoning number of counseling centers that helped prepare women for jobs. In their own words, women explain some of these influences:

In Minneapolis, a twenty-six-year-old mother of three took a clerical job after her husband left her. "I guess women's lib had something to do with it. I sure don't let a man push me around."

And another, this one a California mother whose four children ranged in age from eleven to fifteen, who went back to work as a bookkeeper: "After staying home with four kids for twenty-four hours a day, I wanted some adult companionship, a feeling of accomplishment. Having the cleanest floor on the block isn't the greatest thing that can happen to you."

And in South Orange, New Jersey, the wife of a high-school coach explained why she sought employment in a university library: "I went back—not for the money, but for *me*."

Yet in the midst of this profound revolution in mores, morals, values—a time of rising expectations for women, of possibilities for individual and collective growth—baffling dilemmas and unresolved conflicts haunt our society.

On the most basic level, there is a troubled economy. While during the years 1976 and 1977 some five hundred thousand new jobs were created, this increase does not begin to absorb the new workers now entering the job market, nor does it take up the slack in a country where nearly one out of nine people seeking work cannot find it. America's unemployment rates are the highest since the Great Depression of the 1930's; more important is the fact that the unemployment rates are "pocketed"— not evenly distributed. While men's unemployment rates hover at about 5.5 percent, women's are nearly double, and among minority groups and, particularly, youths, the rate jumps to nearly 40 percent! Hardest hit are young people between sixteen and nineteen, who are out of school, out of work, and generally out of luck in the job market.

A second major problem is that the institutions in society still serve an earlier era. For example, over four and a half million American women with children under the age of six have jobs. About half of these women are middle class; they presumably could afford to pay for child care. For some of them—and for nearly *all* poor mothers—the picture is bleak. At present, licensed centers (all but two states have minimum standards and require licensing) can take care of only about five hundred thousand children, less than 12 percent of the need. A handful of these are run by government, church, or charitable groups; 60 percent are commercial enterprises, where the emphasis is often on profit rather than on good care for children. Centers are often poorly equipped and understaffed.

Other remnants of a time in which men "took care" of women are our Social Security laws, pension plans, disability insurance coverage, income tax regulations. Under Social Security laws, married working women ordinarily do not realize anything on the money they have contributed throughout their working years, for given the choice Social Security offers—a part of a husband's pension or all of their own—most women do better accepting the wife's portion. This means that women who have worked most of their lives do no better than those who have not—an obvious inequality. More than that, Social Security provisions do not take into account women's split careers. While men are given "credit"—which translates to mean "dollars"—for (salaried!) time spent in the armed services, women are not credited with years at no salary spent at home taking care of children.

Nor do pension plans currently take into consideration women's greater mobility in employment—the fact that women follow their husbands' needs to change locations—nor other aspects of women's working patterns. Income tax regulations, too, although they have undergone revision recently, still offer only partial and conditional exemption for child care for working mothers. But undoubtedly the most stunning blow to working women came in December 1976, with the decision by the Supreme Court regarding disability insurance for absences caused by pregnancy. Rejecting the rulings by six United States Courts of Appeals that for an employer to cover a broad range of other disabilities while disallowing pregnancy violates Title VII of the Civil Rights Act of 1964, the Supreme Court ruled in favor of private insurance companies. This decision did more than place the financial burden of childbearing solely on individual women—it cast doubt on the use of Title VII itself! In the words of Susan Rose, an attorney for the American Civil Liberties Union, "The United States Supreme Court has legislated sex discrimination."

In other areas, too, in which the nation should be moving forward for broader, more progressive accommodation, the status quo is maintained—or worse, we are moving backward! The escalating costs of medical care and education and welfare programs have been met with cutbacks. In 1976, for example, there were nearly one-fourth fewer teachers in New York City than five years earlier. Aside from the effect upon the generation now being schooled, this is a real blow to women, for teaching remains the major profession to engage them. In the same way, trimming social-welfare programs also means that women in professions such as psychology and sociology are increasingly unemployed.

Perhaps the worst part of cutting back social services is that this comes at a time when, following a long-term trend, fewer people need to be employed to manufacture goods. Technology continues to eliminate workers in manufacturing, and now computer technology is beginning to take its toll of the large body of clerical workers who are primarily women. As computerized typewriters, bookkeeping machinery, technology that makes it possible for consumers to pay bills by telephone, and other cybernetic advances develop, fewer people will be needed to do office work. This diminishing of the need for women engaged in manufacturing, and now in clerical work as well, creates a gap that can be filled only by developing *more, not fewer,* jobs in the social services. To replace jobs lost to increased technology requires imagination, foresight—perhaps revolutionary new thinking—that our society has not yet caught up to.

What are the solutions for what is, at best, a mixed outlook for working people in general, and working women in particular? Some of the answers may be here in embryo form in our own society. For others, we might look to the experiences of other developed nations.

The need for revision in Social Security laws is long overdue. Various proposals have been made. Among them is the concept of viewing a working husband and wife as a team, so that a couple could toss their earnings into a joint pool, allowing them to receive 150 percent of the benefits of combined earnings—or 75 percent for each partner. This means that women's earnings would be used to bring increased advantages. A second proposal, following European practice, would be to allow women "baby years"—thus minimizing the differences between men's steadier work patterns and the interrupted ones of women.

If working mothers are not to be penalized for having and rearing children, some efforts must be made to spread the financial burdens and the work burdens. A program that is meeting with success in Sweden is an innovative twist on Sweden's long-accepted maternity-leave plan; a combination of generous government grants and modest contributions from employers guarantees about ninety-five percent of the *husband's* salary while he stays home for up to seven months after the couple's baby is born!

The Swedish paternity program does more than allow the wife to continue her own career without a lengthy interruption. It changes the concept of child rearing from the traditional view that it was a mother's responsibility to the idea that parenthood is a joint endeavor. More than that, it means that children have *two* parents who are fully involved, for as a Swedish father explained: "If you don't achieve contact with children in the early months, you can't catch up. Once you start, it's easy to continue."

The American practice of largely ignoring the needs of the children of working mothers can be reversed in other ways too. Women themselves must establish government child care as an important priority. One possibility includes the use of public schools for lengthened after-school care for children in the primary grades.

The weighty problem of providing employment for the nearly two million American young people between sixteen and nineteen who are jobless needs possibly radical solutions. Robert T. Hall, Executive Director of the Manpower Policy Commission, believes that the problem could be attacked effectively by adding about a billion dollars to improve youth job programs under the Comprehensive Employment and Training Act and other Federal legislation. Currently two billion dollars are being spent annually on these programs.

One proposal along these lines, advocated by Sar A. Levitan, Director of George Washington University's Center for Social Policy Studies, would revamp the Job Corps, a program begun under President Lyndon Johnson's "war on poverty" that was cut in half during the administration of President Richard Nixon. Mr. Levitan suggested that it be restored to its old level of forty-five thousand jobs and expanded to keep young people in training programs for at least six months. Another proposal is for sharply expanded apprenticeship programs combined with Federal subsidies.

The most revolutionary program under study is of European origin. An economic recovery law adopted in Belgium in 1976 requires every company or government bureau with more than one hundred employees to expand its payroll by one percent to create probationary jobs for people up to the age of thirty. They are to be kept employed for at least six months at seventy-five percent of the normal starting rate for their jobs. If they are kept another six months, the required minimum goes up to ninety percent.

So far Belgium is showing results so encouraging that the government has just recommended the law be extended to companies with as few as fifty workers. A government subsidy of eight hundred dollars for each young employee is offered to encourage job expansion in smaller businesses. To make room for the new young workers, early retirement of older workers is encouraged through a tax-supported fund that gives them eighty percent of their normal take-home pay until they reach the standard pension age of sixty-five for men and sixty for women. Employers are then obliged to take one young employee for every oldster who leaves.

Perhaps the most important resource that working women have in recognizing women's specific needs and offering working solutions for a country during a major period of transition is women themselves.

Behind us is a long tradition of foresighted women who opened the professions to their sisters, who founded colleges and universities to make higher education co-educational, who penetrated the bastions of trade labor unions, who brought into trade, commerce, and industry the concept of the worker as a full human being with needs and rights, who fought for nearly a century to gain full citizenship for women—civil rights, property rights, the long-coveted right to the ballot.

Today's women who carry forward the banner include the feminists who place their hopes and direct their efforts toward the passage of an Equal Rights Amendment to the Constitution, which will forever guarantee women that "Equality of rights under the law shall not be denied or abridged by the United States or by any State on account of sex"; the women who have, against the odds of discrimination, steadily fought their way into leadership positions in government and public life, and once there brought women's own experiences into legislation and to institutions which determine social and economic policy; working women themselves, millions of them, whose very presence in the labor market establishes them as the core of America's progress and productivity.

For each of these women there is a vital task ahead: to help create a climate in which *every* young woman today can develop along lines which best express her individual abilities, talents, and vision—in a society which values and rewards her contribution.

Bibliography

Baxandall, Ros, et al. *American Women: A Documentary History*. New York: Random House, Inc., 1976.

Bird, Caroline, and Babette Ashby. "Do Working Wives Have Better Marriages?" *Family Circle*, November 1976.

Bird, Caroline, with Sara Welles. *Born Female*. New York: David McKay Company, Inc., 1968, 1974.

Brooks, Thomas R. *Toil and Trouble: A History of American Labor*. New York: Dell Publishing Company, Inc., 1964, 1972.

Clinton, Audrey. "The Paper Historian." *Newsday*, November 20, 1975.

Dexter, Elizabeth W. *Colonial Women of Affairs: Women in Business and the Professions in America before 1776*. Boston: Houghton Mifflin Company, 1931.

Dye, Nancy Schrom. "Creating A Feminist Alliance: Sisterhood and Class Conflict in the New York Women's Trade Union League, 1903–1914." *Feminist Studies*, Vol. 2, Number 2/3, 1975.

Epstein, Cynthia Fuchs. *Woman's Place: Options and Limits in Professional Careers*. Berkeley and Los Angeles: University of California Press, 1970.

Equal Pay. United States Department of Labor, Employment Standards Administration. Washington, D.C.: U.S. Government Printing Office, 1974.

Flexner, Eleanor. *Century of Struggle: The Women's Rights Movement in the United States.* New York: Atheneum Publishers, 1968.

Fourth Annual Report of the Committee of Labor. United States Bureau of Labor. Washington, D.C.: reprint of 1888 ed.

Friedan, Betty. *The Feminine Mystique.* New York: W. W. Norton & Company, Inc., 1963.

Ginzberg, Eli, et al. *Life Styles of Educated Women.* New York: Columbia University Press, 1966.

Gordon, Anna A. *The Beautiful Life of Frances E. Willard.* Chicago: The Women's Temperance Publishing Association, 1898. Reprinted by Peter Wolff.

Harris, Janet. *The Long Freedom Road: The Civil Rights Story.* New York: McGraw-Hill, Inc., 1967.

———. *A Single Standard.* New York: McGraw-Hill, Inc., 1971.

Jabs, Cynthia. "Making Manager a Neuter Term." *The New York Times,* May 2, 1976.

Josephson, Hannah. *Golden Threads: New England's Mill Girls and Magnates.* New York: Russell & Russell, 1949.

Kleiman, Dena. "How Pioneer Women Lived." *The New York Times,* October 17, 1975.

MacLean, Annie Marion. *Wage-Earning Women.* New York: The MacMillan Company, 1910 and 1974.

Mitchell, Joyce Slayton. *Other Choices for Becoming a Woman.* New York: Dell Publishing Company, Inc., 1975.

Peabody, Lucy W. *A Wider World for Women.* Westwood, N.J.: Fleming H. Revell Company, 1936.

Quarles, Benjamin. *The Negro in the Civil War.* Boston: Little, Brown and Company, 1953.

Riley, Edward M., and Charles E. Hatch, Jr., eds. *James Towne in the Words of Contemporaries.* Washington, D.C.: National Park Service Source Book Series No. 5, revised 1955.

Smuts, Robert W. *Women and Work in America.* New

York: Schocken Books, Inc., 1971.

Sterba, James P. "Amid the Grime, A Woman Earns a Job Offshore." *The New York Times*, December 30, 1975.

Stevens, William K. "Blue Collar Women—Pioneers on the Assembly Line in Detroit." *The New York Times*, March 29, 1976.

U.S. Working Women: A Chartbook. United States Department of Labor, Bureau of Labor Statistics, Bulletin 1880. Washington, D.C.: 1975.

Women Workers Today. Women's Bureau, Employment Administration, United States Department of Labor. Washington, D.C.: 1974.

Yellen, Samuel. *American Labor Struggles, 1877–1934*. New York: Monad Press, 1974.

Index

Format by Joyce Hopkins
Set in 11 pt Janson
Composed, printed and bound by Vail–Ballou Press, Inc.
HARPER & ROW, PUBLISHERS, INCORPORATED

DATE DUE			
MAY 20			
FEB 20			
MAR 15			
5/4/98			
30 505 JOSTEN'S